Household Hints

HUNDREDS OF EVERYDAY USES

Publisher's Notes:
All possible care has been exercised by the author and publisher to ensure that the tips and remedies included in this guide are basic, simple and safe. However, it is still important to note that all uses of traditional remedies and ingredients should be practised with caution and a doctor's, or relevant professional's, advice should be sought if in any doubt.

Please note also that the measurements provided in this book are presented as metric/imperial/US practical equivalents.

This is a **STAR FIRE** book
First published in 2009

Publisher and Creative Director: Nick Wells
Project Editors: Polly Prior and Cat Emslie
Picture Research: Katie Pimlott and Cat Emslie
Art Director: Mike Spender
Layout Design: Dave Jones
Digital Design and Production: Chris Herbert
Proofreader: Dawn Laker
Indexer: Helen Snaith

09 11 13 12 10

1 3 5 7 9 10 8 6 4 2

This edition first published in 2009 by
STAR FIRE
Crabtree Hall, Crabtree Lane
Fulham, London SW6 6TY
United Kingdom

www.star-fire.co.uk

Star Fire is part of The Foundry Creative Media Co. Ltd

ISBN 978-1-84786-520-5

A CIP Record for this book is available from the British Library upon request.

Printed in China

The following images are © Foundry Arts: 118, 125, 139t, 139b. All other pictures are courtesy of Shutterstock and © the following photographers: 1 & 30 Brian Chase; 3 & 4t & 74 & 80, 60 GWImages; 4l & 43 easyshoot; 4r & 78 Sergey Kartashov; 5l & 108 XPhantom; 5r & 189 Olga Solovei; 6b ZQFotography; 6t & 52 & 54 Shantell photographe; 7, 154 Stephen Coburn; 8 Elena Schweitzer; 9, 151 Deborah Reny; 10 maigi; 11 Pinkcandy; 12 & 17 Sergey Lukyanov; 13b Hallgerd; 13t Rayisa Nalivayko; 14 Dmitry Takunin; 16, 26 Ragne Kabanova; 18 & 19 Daniel Goodings; 20 Shvaygert Ekaterina; 22, 33 Elena Talberg; 23, 40 Anthony Berenyi; 24 & 25 MalibuBooks; 27 Cecilia Lim H M; 28 Olga Chernetskaya; 29 Marek CECH; 31 TheSupe87; 32 & 36 Thomas M Perkins; 35 Gina Sanders; 38, 156 Kapu; 41 Johnna Evang Nonboe; 42 & 44b & 192, 166 matka_Wariatka; 44t Shannon West; 45 Carsten Reisinger; 46 & 47 Perkus; 48 Magdalena Kucova; 50 WilleeCole; 51 Jacques Kloppers; 53b, 117 Morgan Lane Photography; 53t Eky Chan; 55 Anne Kitzman; 56 Ruta Saulyte-Laurinaviciene; 57 GreenStockCreative; 58b dakolix; 58t Natalia V Guseva; 59 jirkaejc; 61 Nikolay Okhitin; 62 & 63 ewa b; 64b Dmitriy Shironosov; 64t Rafa Irusta; 65 dalereardon; 66 cen; 67 David B Peterson; 68 tim elliot; 70, 101 Anthony Harris; 72 & 82, 174t Andrjuss; 73, 77 Petoo; 75 Camara Escura; 76 Imgorthand; 79 Losevsky Pavel; 83 Steve Cukrov; 84 Adrian Britton; 85 STILLFX; 90 Cynthia Farmer; 91 Keir Davis; 92 Brian Weed; 93 Konstantin Sutyagin; 94 & 95 Mawroidis Kamila; 96 8781118005; 97 Peter Clark; 98 & 104 Kutlayev Dmitry; 99 guidocava; 100 Arvind Balaraman; 102 silver-john; 103 Olegusk; 105 mates; 106 Nancy Tripp; 110 & 111 Phase4Photography; 113 rodho; 114 ivaskes; 115 Kerry Garvey; 116 & 136 Paul Maguire; 119 Szymon Apanowicz; 121 AGITA; 122 Dewayne Flowers; 123 KSLight; 124, 183b Monkey Business Images; 126 & 131 Pavelk; 127b 833379753; 127t PeterG; 128 Hitdelight; 129 Robyn Mackenzie; 130 Marie C. Fields; 133 Mike Flippo; 135 Richard Goldberg; 137 TonyB.; 140 Jason Nemeth; 141 Hannamariah; 142 & 149, 146 Ingrid Balabanova; 143 Feng Yu; 144 Daisy Daisy; 145 R. MACKKAY PHOTOGRAPHY; 147 Nic Neish; 148 CJPhoto; 150 Lorraine Kourafas; 153 Sandra Kemppainen; 157 Tania Zbrodko; 160 vgstudio; 161 Lilia Beck; 162 AVAVA; 163 Tihis; 165 Ronald Sumners; 168b Navita; 168t Afina_ok; 170 & 173t Dolnikov; 171 Xalanx; 172 Tootles; 173b barbaradudzinska; 174b Birute Vijeikiene; 175 rebvt; 176 Kimberly Hall; 177, 179 greenland; 178 & 181 Quayside; 180 Kiri Vaclavek; 183t Juliya W. Shumskaya; 184 & 185 Carlos Moura; 186 Victor Burnside; 187 anna karwowska; 188l Kruchankova Maya; 188r Leah-Anne Thompson

Household Hints

HUNDREDS OF EVERYDAY HINTS

Maria Costantino

STAR FIRE

Contents

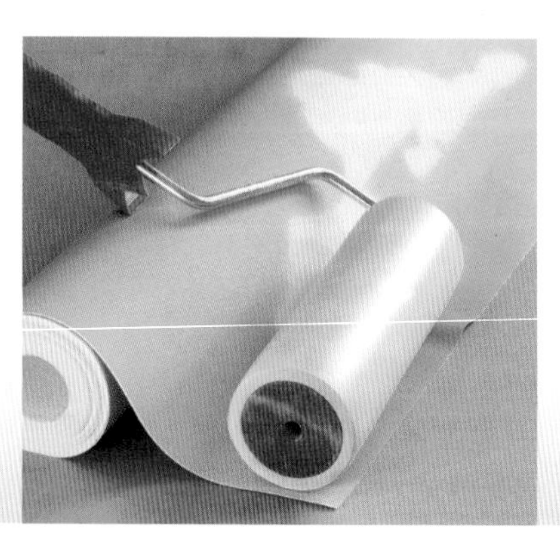

Introduction

These days, it is almost impossible to pick up a newspaper or switch on the television or radio without being reminded that the economy is in trouble and planet Earth itself in danger. Consequently, many people are rethinking the way we run and look after our planet, lives and ourselves by introducing common-sense energy saving measures, turning to tried and trusted recipes, re-using, recycling and making do and mending. This does not mean we are lowering our standards, but just that to maintain existing standards we have to work a little harder, think a little longer and consider the impact of our actions a little more than we used to.

In Landfill Site, Out of Mind?

The one thing we are all experts in is consuming: we have one product to clean this, a cream for that and a scented spray to disguise this cocktail of chemicals so we can convince ourselves that our homes and bodies are germ-free, clean and safe. We then dump the containers in landfill sites to leach into the soil and into water courses. There are eco-friendly alternatives on the market, but these green products can be expensive and their promotion can appear as a cynical marketing strategy, especially when they are produced by the same manufacturers who make the more polluting products too. The important thing to remember is that people looked after their homes, clothes and bodies *before* such products were manufactured. It is important that we tap into this wealth of knowledge before it is lost.

(Grand)Mother Knows Best

For a long time down-home wisdom was derided as old-fashioned and dismissed as old wives' (and husbands') tales, and the older generation were scoffed at for being set in their ways. On the one hand, grandparents were laughed at for keeping bits of string, jam jars and brown paper; on the other hand, they were celebrated because no one could ever bake bread, knit a scarf, grow vegetables, tell a story or make a toy out of wood like they could. Grandma and Grandpa knew that a routine was the best way to keep a house and garden shipshape; that vinegar and newspaper was the best thing for cleaning windows and mirrors; that bicarbonate of soda banished smells from larders, fridges and smelly shoes; that lemon juice cleaned brass and copper, removed rust and stains from marble and 'bleached' wooden chopping boards clean.

An Invaluable Resource

In this book you will find lots of easy-to-follow hints, tips and ideas to help you care for your home. You do not need to buy expensive products, in fact you will find you have most of them in your kitchen cupboards already; others are widely available and cost very little. And don't worry: you won't become an obsessive cleaner, either! But you will find that you can save yourself some time, energy and money by getting organized, clearing out the clutter in your life, organizing your wardrobe and drawers so you can find outfits easily, making a few adjustments to the way you use appliances and utilities, and keep everything from your floors, walls and furnishings to your clothes, skin, teeth and hair shiny, bright and clean and looking new for much longer.

You never know, but you may find that you enjoy yourself too, and you can look forward to the day when you too can pass on the knowledge to the next generation! Fashions and fads may come and go, but good old common sense will always be in style, so get started now!

Cleaning

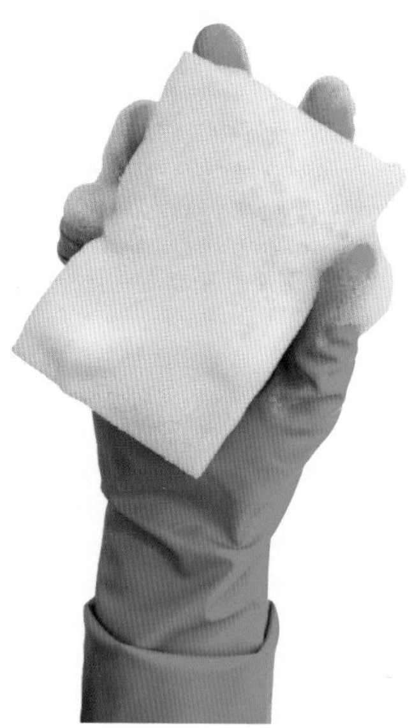

Kitchens

Big or small, kitchens are the engine rooms of our homes and the place where family and friends naturally seem to converge. Consequently, kitchens need to be safe and hygienic, and that means a thorough cleaning routine should be introduced and followed. Washing up is just a small part of the process: the work surfaces, sinks and plugholes, as well as the domestic appliances that are used daily, need to be cared for.

Washing Up

Due Process

Do the washing up straight away: dried and hardened-on food takes longer to remove. And there's an order to washing up: glasses first; then cutlery, then crockery, then pots and pans – saving the greasiest for last. And do not waste washing-up liquid: wipe the plates and pots first with a paper towel – or even a sheet of newspaper. Add just a few drops of washing-up liquid – too much will just produce bubbles – to water as hot as is comfortable and add some elbow grease.

Naturally Effective Bicarbonate and Vinegar

Clean worktops and surfaces with a damp cloth dipped in bicarbonate of soda, while adding white vinegar to the rinse water will remove any alkaline soap residue from the surface of crockery. Cloudy drinking glasses can often be made clear again by soaking them for an hour in warm white vinegar and scrubbing gently with a nylon net or soft dish brush. Undiluted white vinegar at five per cent acidity is effective against *E.Coli*, *Salmonella* and *Staphylococcus:* use it to clean wooden and plastic cutting boards, butcher's blocks and non-marble counter tops before and after food preparation.

Roll Out the Kitchen Roll

Remove stains from ceramic butler's or Belfast sinks by placing a layer of paper towels in the base and saturating with bleach. Leave for five minutes, remove the paper and rinse clean. Clean can openers by feeding a piece of paper towel through the jaws.

Spotless Sinks

Clean stainless steel sinks and taps with a cloth soaked in warm, soapy water. Rinse with clean water and wipe dry. Do not use bleach on stainless steel sinks because it can cause surface pitting. Half a lemon rubbed around the sink – in particular around the plughole – will help remove limescale deposits.

Appliances

Before you clean any electrical appliance, switch off the power (at the mains in the case of hard-wired appliances such as dishwashers and electric stoves which are wired into fused connection units). Portable electric appliances like kettles and toasters should be unplugged from their sockets.

Thrills and Spills

Clean as you go: keep a damp cloth handy to wipe up cooking spills so they do not get dried or baked on to the hob. Treat spills in the oven during cooking by sprinkling with salt and then wiping off when the oven is cool. Treat stubborn dried-on spills – and any chrome or stainless steel parts – with a paste of bicarbonate of soda and water. Leave it on for 10–15 minutes and then wipe off with a soft cloth. This also works well on those brown streaks on oven windows, but only do this when the oven is cool!

Microwaves and Toasters

Clean and deodorize your microwave by placing a heatproof container of white vinegar or water with three of four lemon slices added, in the centre of the machine. Turn the machine on to the highest setting for one minute and then wipe the walls and ceiling of the microwave with a soft cloth. Keep toasters working safely and efficiently – and avoid setting off smoke alarms – by regularly removing loose breadcrumbs.

Limescale Removal

Minimize limescale build-up in kettles by not leaving water sitting in it. A traditional method to reduce scale is to pop a rough seashell into the kettle: the shell attracts the lime so it does not fur up the element.

Melting Glaciers

A fridge whose freezer compartment contains a glacier is inefficient and needs defrosting. Remove all food (ask a neighbour to keep it for you, or store in cool bags or wrapped in a thick blanket of newspaper), turn off the power and unplug the fridge. Put a towel or sheets of newspaper on both the floor of the fridge and the kitchen floor, and a washing-up bowl on one of the shelves. This will catch and contain the melting ice. Leave the door open while the fridge defrosts; if you want to speed things up, aim a hairdryer at the glacier (but keep the heat off plastic parts of the fridge). Once defrosted, clean the inside of the fridge with a mix

of bicarbonate of soda and water. Avoid using detergents or washing-up liquid as these can leave food-tainting odours. Wipe or brush a little glycerine (available from pharmacists) over the inside of freezer compartments after it has been defrosted: the next time you need to defrost, the ice will come away in sheets, speeding up the whole process – this works in main freezers too.

Whiter than White

The exterior casings of white goods – washing machines, fridges, freezers and dishwashers – can be kept from yellowing by wiping with a solution of ½ cup of household bleach, ½ cup of bicarbonate of soda and 8 cups of water. Rinse off afterwards with clean water. Touch up scratches and marks on fridge and freezer doors by using matching car body-work touch-up paint which comes in handy pen-style applicators.

Odours

Absorb It, Banish It

An egg cup or small plastic container filled with bicarbonate of soda placed in your fridge and discreetly behind the toilet will absorb and neutralize odours. A small piece of school blackboard chalk in your bread bin will absorb any moisture and keep the contents fresher for longer. Chalk also stops silver tarnishing in drawers. As for unpleasant bathroom smells – they can be banished by striking a match.

Mustard with Everything

Deodorize vacuum flasks and other types of closed jugs and containers by rinsing out with water to which a little mustard (any kind!) has been added.

Lemon Aid

Lingering onion, garlic and fish smells on food preparation surfaces and chopping boards can be removed by rubbing half a lemon dipped in salt over the area. And waste disposal units can be kept fragrant if you regularly feed citrus peel through them.

Stinky Bins

The source of most suspiciously stinky smells will be the waste bin. Rinse out empty tins, jars and bottles for recycling and do not put newly brewed hot teabags in the bin – they raise the temperature inside, cause steam and condensation and consequently make the bin into an indoor compost heap. After you have emptied the bin, wash it inside and out (and the lid too), let it dry and sprinkle the insides with some bicarbonate of soda before you put in a fresh bin liner.

Bathrooms

Restoring order in bathrooms is like cleaning your teeth: you need to make it a habit! Five minutes each day is all it takes to keep a clean bathroom if you get into the routine of cleaning up after yourself each time you use it. Wipe away water, soap and toothpaste splashes; squeegee the shower and rinse out the bathtub; and give the loo a 'flush-brush-flush' clean in the morning before you leave the house to help reduce unsightly stains.

Lavatories

Lovely Loos

Do not use bleach as a lavatory cleaner on a regular basis: this can cause the glaze on the bowl to craze and crack, leading to the build-up of hard-to-shift stains. If your lavatory bowl is in poor condition, it means you are harbouring germs and faecal spores so consider replacing it – and get one that is also water efficient.

There are some environmentally friendly lavatory cleaners that are also cheaper than proprietary products whose power lies in them being mildly acidic: white vinegar or a large bottle of cheap cola drink. Scoop the water out of the toilet bowl and replace with the white vinegar or cola and leave for an hour or so before flushing.

Two or three effervescent Vitamin C tablets or denture cleaning tablets dropped into the bowl and left overnight are also pretty effective toilet cleaners.

Limescale

Limescale build-up in toilet bowls is unsightly and, because it clogs up the system, can make for inefficient and noisy flushing. If all liquid attempts to remove it have failed, you might need to remove it manually. Do not, however, reach for a screwdriver or any other metal tool to scrape with; use a piece of brick instead. The brick is harder than the limescale so will rub it off but, more importantly, the brick is softer than the porcelain of the loo bowl, so it will not scratch into it.

Showers & Tiles

De-Scale it!

De-scale showerheads as the holes in the head can get blocked and can lead to the water backing up in your water pipes. If the showerhead unscrews, take it off (taking care not to lose the rubber washer inside) and soak the head in a bowl of white vinegar. Scrub into the holes with an old toothbrush. If the head does not unscrew, fill a polythene bag with white vinegar and fasten it around the showerhead and let it soak. You can also use this method for bath and basin taps.

Dry it Out

Use a squeegee to remove excess water from shower cubicles and panels. Leave shower panels and screens open (but close shower curtains) after showering to allow them to dry.

Mildew

Washable shower curtains can be revived by adding ½ cup of white vinegar to the rinse water; this also helps to kill off any mildew. If you use a washing machine, take the curtain out before the spin cycle so it does not crease. Hang it up to air dry instead. Zap mould or mildew in shower cubicles – especially around the edges, the joins where the waterproof sealant is and in the base tracks for sliding screens – by spraying with neat white vinegar.

Tiles

Bathroom tiles and shower panels can also be de-scaled with white vinegar. Apply it neat with a cloth and leave on for 10 minutes before rinsing off. Grotty grout is both unsightly and harbours germs: oddly, the best grout cleaner is the foaming type of oven cleaner. Make sure the bathroom is well ventilated – open the window (if there is one) and the door. Wear rubber gloves and spray the oven cleaner on to a small section of grout at a time, count to three quickly and then wipe off and rinse straight away.

Banish Mould

Moisture on walls and ceilings can be a particular problem in bathrooms, and small, enclosed or poorly ventilated areas can encourage mould growth. Because oil repels water, try wiping a little baby oil over the bathroom walls and ceiling once in a while.

Taps & Bath Tubs

Stop the Drip

A dripping tap can leave limescale deposits and cause rust marks. It also wastes valuable water, so replace the washer and stop the drip.

Spit and Polish

Clean chrome taps with a little household ammonia mixed with water. Rinse with clean water and polish dry. No ammonia? Then rub with a damp cloth and a little toothpaste instead. Do not forget to clean behind taps. Use an old toothbrush to get into the hard-to-reach areas.

Rinse as you Go

Rinsing the tub after bathing will get rid of most residual dirt, bath salts or oil-based bath preparations. For a thorough clean up, use a non-abrasive cleaner for vitreous enamel, acrylic, cast iron or steel baths and pay attention to any scummy tide marks. Glass fibre baths (and shower trays) are best cleaned with a simple solution of washing-up liquid.

Rusting Away

Rust marks on old cast-iron baths can often be bleached out by applying a paste of cream of tartar or one of salt and lemon juice. If these fail, and only if your bath is white, try rubbing a little hydrogen peroxide on the stain.

Down the Plughole

The plughole is where the gunk goes: soap, shower gels, bath oil and toothpaste, dead skin, loose hairs and dirt all go there, but a 'fur ball' of hair makes for an excellent particle trap so it needs to be removed: put 1 cup of washing soda over the plughole and pour a kettle full of boiling water over it.

General Household

If you leave it until you absolutely must clean, you will find the job takes longer and is much harder to do. Make a habit of cleaning up and tidying as you go: wipe up spills and wash dishes before you run out of clean plates; empty the kitchen bin daily and get rid of yesterday's newspapers and junk mail. Simple things like this mean that a good clean need only happen once a week or so and a spring clean takes place only in spring!

Floors

Different Chores for Different Floors

Revive old linoleum by mopping with a mixture of equal parts milk and turpentine and then rubbing with a soft, warm cloth.

Do not use solvent-based cleaners on vinyl flooring as it can strip off the protective surface. Instead, use a warm water solution of household detergent and rinse with clean water. Keep your mop as dry as possible when mopping adhesive vinyl tiles to prevent water from getting between the seams and causing the corners to lift and curl.

Never soak wooden floors: the boards swell and then can warp when they dry out. Do not use very hot water either: this can make the wood soft and pulpy. Sweep or vacuum sanded and sealed wooden floors and, if you must wash them, use a well-wrung mop and a solution of household detergent.

Stain Removal

Scuff marks on vinyl flooring often come off if you rub a pencil eraser over them. Alternatively, wipe the scuff firmly with a dry cloth and a pea-sized blob of toothpaste.

Treat oil and grease stains on wooden floors with a paste of Fuller's Earth mixed with soap and water. Apply to the stain and leave it for a couple of days. Wipe away and rub the wood very gently along the grain with fine sandpaper. Repeat the process until the stain has lifted.

Blot up stains on carpets immediately: work from the outside edge of the stain to the middle so you don't spread it wider – and do not rub or brush the stain.

White wine spillages need blotting and dousing with soda or sparkling mineral water. Red wine spills need treating with white wine: blot up as much of the red as you can with a clean, dry cloth. Put a second clean, dry cloth over the stain and pour some white wine on to it. Wait for the red wine stain to be soaked up, blot the area again and rinse with lukewarm water before a final blotting.

Glycerine is an extremely effective tea-stain remover: work it gently into the stain and then blot with warm water. No glycerine? Try blotting with lemon juice.

Carpets and Rugs

Professionals advise passing the vacuum cleaner over a carpet at least eight times for a real, deep down clean. After you have vacuumed the top sides, loose-laid carpets and rugs should also be vacuumed on their reverse sides.

Harness static electricity to remove fluff and hairs from carpets: dampen an old nylon stocking or tights leg, put it over your hand and wipe it over the carpet.

Raise the pile on carpets crushed by furniture by placing a small ice cube in the dent. Let it melt, leave the wet patch to dry, then finish by vacuuming to 'suck' the tufts upright.

Make a room look ten times tidier by combing the fringe on rugs with a wide-tooth comb so it lies straight.

Upholstery

Vacuum it

Use your vacuum cleaner on upholstered furniture to remove loose dirt, dust and crumbs – and use the crevice tool to get into the nooks and crannies. Draw the curtains and vacuum them to keep them dust free for longer. And don't forget the pelmet: inside and out.

Cushions

Turn cushions over and alter their positions on sofas and chairs to even out wear. And do not tidy newspapers away underneath cushions: the printer's ink will migrate on to the fabric!

Hair Removal

Animal hairs seem immune to vacuuming: try running a rubber glove over the cushions to bunch up the hairs for lifting off. You can also lift pet hairs off upholstery with parcel tape: make a big loop sticky side outwards, slip your hand though and roll the tape over the hairy spots. (This works pretty well on clothes too.)

Check the Label

Check the care label on upholstered furnishings before you buy or use any preparatory cleaners: W indicates a water-based or foam upholster shampoo can be used; S means use only a water-free dry cleaning solvent; S-W means you can use an upholstery shampoo or water-free solvent, and X means that you should only vacuum: no cleaning agents should be used at all.

Grease

Shiny, greasy hand (and head) marks on the arms and backs of chairs and sofas can be treated with a clean cloth dampened with a solution of 2 teaspoons white vinegar mixed in 250 ml/8 fl oz/1 cup lukewarm water. Test an inconspicuous area first for colour fastness and use as little moisture on the cloth as possible to avoid wetting the padding or stuffing.

Windows, Mirrors & Glass

Watch the Weather

Clean windows on a dry but dull day: direct sunshine will bathe the glass in light and heat and it will dry too fast, leaving streaks. Do not clean windows on very cold or frosty days: both the glass and the putty will be brittle and you could break the glass, or even push panes out of their frames. (If you do break anything, pick up fine slivers, splinters or fragments of glass by pressing a slice of bread against them.)

A Clean Solution

Add a good dash of vinegar to clean water to make a cheap but effective window cleaning solution: it cuts through grease and dirt and keeps flies away in hot weather. For really dirty windows, try a solution of 1 teaspoon household ammonia and 1 tablespoon methylated spirits in 500 ml/18 fl oz/2 cups water. You can decant this into a labelled spray bottle for easy use.

Smear Free

Locate smears on windows by polishing with brown paper or scrunched up newspaper: use horizontal strokes inside and vertical strokes outside – then you will know which side the smear is on!

Steamy Windows

A few drops of glycerine on a cloth wiped over bathroom mirrors and windows will stop them from steaming up. Alternatively, run the cut side of a potato across windows and mirrors – London cabbies swear by this to keep their windscreens clear.

Laundry & Clothes Care

Washing

Looking after your clothes means you will always look your best and will prolong the life of your wardrobe. Whether you wash by hand or use a washing machine, make sure you use the right washing procedure for different types of fabrics, the right water temperature and the right type of soap or detergent. Before you buy new clothes, always look for the international care label. Washing powder or liquid packages also carry care information to help you keep your wardrobe looking good as new.

Laundering

A Happy Machine

To get a clean wash, you need a clean machine: while you can buy proprietary washing machine cleaners – similar to a dishwasher cleaner – these are expensive. Instead, run 4.5 litres (about 1 gallon) of white vinegar through your machine on a warm water setting followed by a rinse cycle. This will cut through the built-up soap residue that can leave a bloom on clothes.

Make sure you periodically check the hoses and connections of your machine: the rubber degrades over time, so check and replace worn fittings before you have a flooded house.

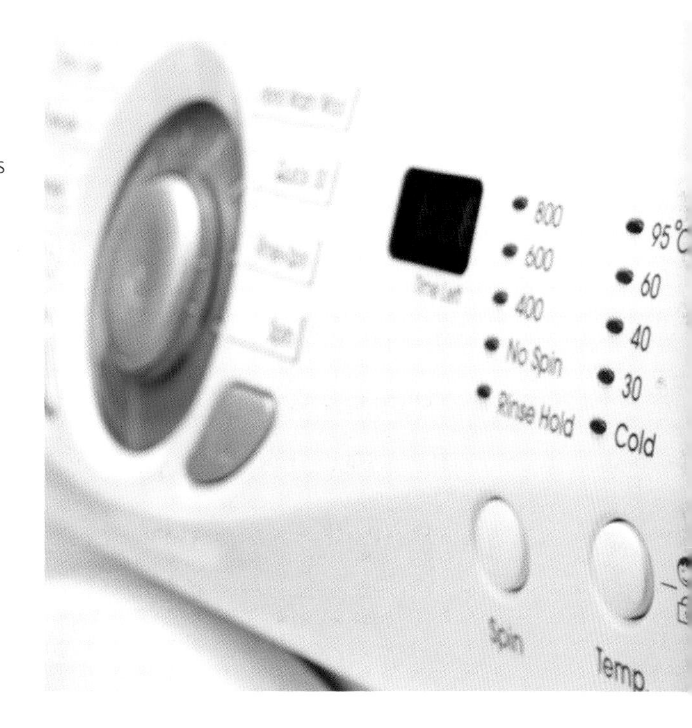

Sorting and Loading Tips

Sort laundry out into piles: white cottons and linens, woollens, non-colour fast items, silk and other delicate fabrics. Wash each pile separately to avoid colour runs and damage.

To stop tangling, shake out and place garments one at a time into washing machines and fasten cuffs to the front buttons of shirts and blouses. And do not overload your washing machine: clothes will come out cleaner if there is room for them to circulate freely.

Rub a Dub Dub

Pre-treat dirty collars and cuffs on shirts by rubbing them with a moistened bar of soap or applying a paste of bicarbonate of soda and white vinegar, and giving them a gentle scrub with an old toothbrush. Rinse and then launder. For oily marks on collars and cuffs try using a blob of your regular shampoo as it is designed to remove oily residues from hair and body.

Soaking

A bathtub is the best place to soak clothes. Try to keep garments immersed during soaks and soak overnight in cold water to avoid setting stains further into the fabric. Do not soak leather, suede, Lycra, flame resistant fabrics or garments with metal trimmings (they'll rust!).

Hand Washing

Sensitive skin? Wear rubber gloves, but make sure the water temperature is not too hot for your laundry.

Gently squeeze water through garments and avoid rubbing, twisting or wringing them – especially if they are made of wool – so they keep their shape.

Do not lift garments out of a sink, bowl or bath when they are soaking wet otherwise you put undue strain on seams and can stretch garments out of shape. Empty the water out of the bowl or basin and press the excess water out of the garment.

Stain Removal

Glycerine as General Stain Remover

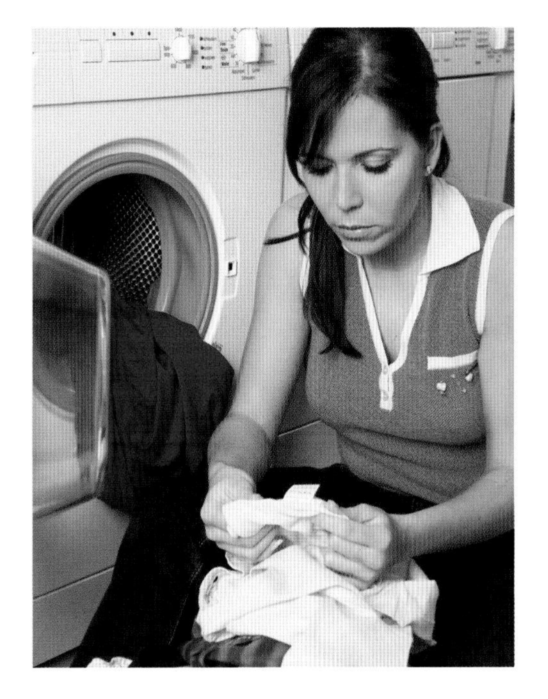

Glycerine softens and loosens dried-in stains. Dilute 1 part glycerine to 2 parts water and apply to the stain. Leave it for an hour before laundering.

Anti-perspirant

Remove anti-perspirant stains by applying a paste of bicarbonate of soda, salt and water with an old toothbrush. Leave the paste on for 30 minutes, then launder as usual.

Blood

A soon as a blood stain occurs, spray with soda water and then apply a paste of cornstarch and water before laundering. Alternatively, try soaking the stain in strongly salted cold water – not hot as this will seal in the stain. Keep changing the brine until the water runs clear and then rub any remaining marks with a paste of salt and water. For dried-on blood stains, soak the garment in a solution of 2 teaspoons ammonia, 500 ml/18 fl oz/2 cups water and a few drops of hydrogen peroxide. Follow the soak with a wash in biological detergent.

Chewing Gum

Chewing gum on clothes is best frozen off. Pick off as much loose gum as you can without damaging the fabric, then put the garment into a plastic bag and place it in the freezer for an hour or so. This should make the remaining gum brittle and easily picked off. Remove any remaining traces by rubbing the stain with a little egg white or soaking in white vinegar before rinsing and laundering.

Candle Wax

Freeze off candle wax too – put the garment in a plastic bag and pop it in the freezer for an hour. Alternatively, sandwich the stain between blotting paper or clean, old t-shirt fabric and run a warm iron over it. Move the blotting paper or fabric around to absorb the wax. You may have to flush out any remaining wax (or its residual colour) with dry-cleaning fluid or a half-and-half mix of methylated spirits and water. Finally, wash the garment in the hottest water it can stand.

Fruit and Grass

Sprinkle salt over fruit stains, rinse in cold water and then launder. If the stain persists, try a little hydrogen peroxide on the stain and launder again.

Rub lemon juice on to grass stains before laundering.

Grease

Greasy stains need to be treated before laundering otherwise they will stick. Dry-cleaning fluid, available in bottles, is really effective at grease removal but do test for colour fastness and do not use on acetate fabrics. Follow the manufacturers' instructions and avoid contact with rubber and plastic materials.

Ink

Ballpoint ink is carried in a very fine suspension of castor oil: start by reducing the stain by rubbing gently with an eraser using a circular motion. Then rub a block of lightly moistened soap over the mark, press the lather through the fabric with your fingers and rinse in warm water. If the fabric is white, you can also try a mix of salt and lemon juice. On dark or coloured clothes, ballpoint pen ink can be removed by soaking the garment in hot (but not boiling) soured milk. It is a slow process but it does work.

Fountain pen ink can be removed by dabbing on rubbing alcohol (available at pharmacists) and blotting with a clean cloth. And stains made by felt tip or marker pens can be treated with a quick spray of hairspray before laundering. Do a spot test first to make sure the hairspray does not lift any colour or leave a stain itself.

Lipstick and Mascara

Lipstick on your collar? Scrape off any excess, then treat by rubbing a little glycerine or even petroleum jelly on to the mark to loosen it before laundering. If this does not work, then you will need a proprietary stain remover or de-greaser followed by a laundering. Mascara stains come off if you rub a little washing-up liquid on to them before laundering.

Tea and Coffee

Fresh coffee and tea stains can be removed by applying a mix of egg yolk and glycerine, then laundering in lukewarm water – not hot or you will end up with a cooked egg stain! Dried-on tea stains should be softened with a solution of equal parts glycerine and warm water and then soaked in a biological detergent. On white cotton, you may have to reach for the bleach.

Tomato Sauce

To remove tomato sauce stains, try rubbing (gently) a good dollop of shaving foam on the stain with your fingers! Rinse off, then launder.

Wine

Wine stains need immediate action: soak white wine stains with soda or mineral water, blot up the excess liquid and launder immediately. Douse red wine stains with white wine, then treat the fabric as if for a white wine stain! If there is no white wine to hand, sprinkle the red wine stain immediately with salt and then wash in cold water and detergent. If the stain remains, try dabbing a paste of cream of tartar and water on it, rinse off, then wash in cold water and detergent.

Bright Whites

Bleach Alternative

You do not need to use chlorine bleach: 2 tablespoons cream of tartar added to a bucket of hot water works just as well – and is kinder to the environment. Let the garments soak in the solution overnight before washing.

Undergarments

White cotton smalls – socks, pants, bras – can be restored to whiteness by placing them in a saucepan, filling with water and adding some lemon slices. Bring the water temperature up to hot and stir the smalls with a clean wooden spoon.

Wool Reviver

Rescue and revive discoloured woollens by soaking overnight in a solution of 1 part hydrogen peroxide and 8 parts cold water. Rinse the garments thoroughly before washing according to the care label.

Curtains

To restore nylon net curtains to whiteness, fill a bath or large bucket with very hot water, add 100 ml/3½ fl oz/1/3 cup dishwasher detergent and 50 ml/2 fl oz/¼ cup household bleach. Allow the mixture to cool to room temperature before soaking the nets for at least 30 minutes, then rinse with cold water. Tip: hang nets up when they are still damp so any creases fall out.

Caring for Colours

Colour Fastness and Preserving Colour

To test for colour fastness, sandwich the garment between white fabric and run a steam iron over a small section: if the dye is transferred to any of the white fabric, then this garment needs to be washed separately and by hand.

Preserve the brightness of coloured garments: before their first wash, soak them in a bucket or bath of water to which you have added a good handful of salt.

Black and Beautiful

Soap build-up can make black garments appear dull: soak them in lukewarm water with a little white vinegar to restore their blackness. Alternatively, machine wash, replacing the detergent with water softener.

Denim

New denim can shed some colour when first washed so soak your jeans for 30 minutes in a bath of 4.5 l/1 gal/4 qts cold water and 50 ml/2 fl oz/¼ cup white vinegar. To stop denim fading too quickly, wash it inside out.

Delicate Fabrics

Silk

Two sugar lumps added to the rinse water will restore the body to silk garments; a few drops of lanolin will also protect and restore silk but, for crisp silk, try adding a dash of white vinegar to the rinse water.

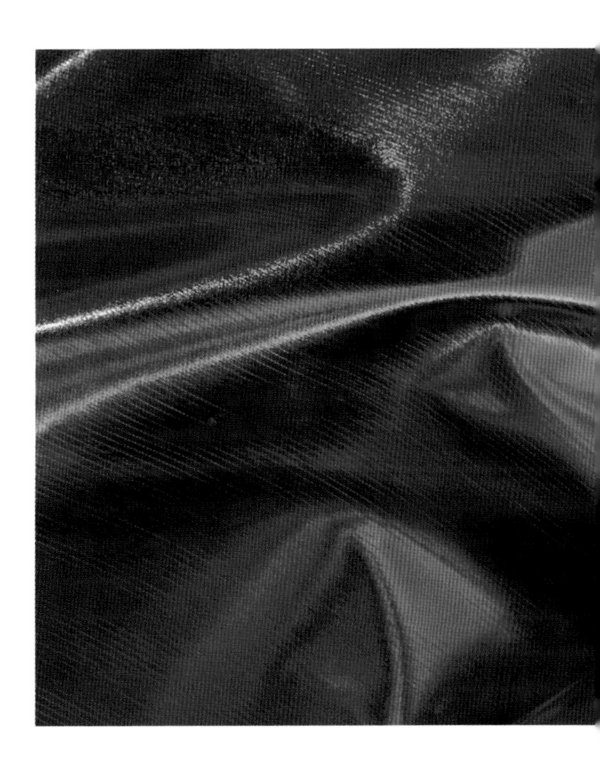

Vintage and Lace

Hand wash delicate, vintage fabrics and lace garments by placing them in a pillowcase: lift and turn the pillowcase, squeezing the water through it before rinsing in the usual way. Vintage clothes that may be a bit on the smelly side can be revived by dissolving three or four crushed aspirins in the rinse water.

Dry-cleaned Clothes

After clothes have been dry-cleaned, rip off the thin plastic cover as soon as possible! Take the clothes off the wire coat hangers and hang them on suitable hangers to air off before putting away. This will get rid of any leftover fumes from the cleaning fluids. Keep the wire hangers, though, they are useful in the garden or for making temporary TV aerials!

Drying & Storing

Line drying saves money and energy. But it is only feasible if it's not raining and you have access to an outside space. You can still air-dry inside on a warm, dry day by using a folding drying rack placed in front of an open window. Clothes in wardrobes and drawers also need ventilation, so make sure there is plenty of space between garments so the air circulates around them. And, if you are putting clothes into storage for next season, avoid moth and mildew damage by making sure they are freshly laundered and absolutely dry.

Drying

Tumble Dryers

Keep light-coloured, fluffy garments – like towels and sweat tops – separate from dark garments in dryers unless you want fluff transferred to your dark clothes!

Make your own fabric softener sheets: put a few drops of liquid fabric softener on a large handkerchief and toss this into the dryer! You can use the hankie-softener at least six times before you need to 're-fresh' it!

If you put two or three clean tennis balls in the dryer along with your linens, you can save 25–50 per cent on drying time. The balls also fluff up towels to a great softness!

Line Drying

To prevent indentation marks by pegs on jumpers, thread a pair of nylon tights through the arms of the jumper, pull the waistband of the tights through the neck of the jumper and attach the pegs to the waistband and feet!

Peg clothes to lines at the garments' strongest points: skirts by the waistband, but trousers by their hems; the weight of the body will help draw out creases and make ironing (and drying) easier.

Storing

Heaven Scent

Freshen your closet and drawers by placing cotton wool balls sprayed with your favourite scent, lavender or clove oil. Let the scented balls dry and pop them into the corners.

Banish smelly shoes: fill an old sock with cat litter or bicarbonate of soda, tie the end closed and place the filled socks into the shoes when you are not wearing them. The litter or bicarbonate of soda absorbs moisture and odours.

Moths

Moths hate lavender: make a little bag or fill the toe of an old sock or pair of tights with dried lavender and hang it inside wardrobe doors. Do not get lavender onto clothes as it can cause holes too. Moths also hate cedar wood: small cedar wood blocks or balls are readily available. Once in a while, give them a light sanding to release the oil that drives moths away. Citrus peel and whole cloves are also excellent moth repellents: if you do not have time to stick cloves into a tangerine, just put some citrus peel and a few cloves into your wardrobe. You can even put some cloves into pockets before you store garments.

Another more pleasant-smelling alternative to mothballs is to shave a bar of soap into slivers and put them into a vented plastic bag. Put the bag in your winter or summer storage trunk before packing away clothes.

Hanging Tips

Shake out and hang up clothes straight away after you have worn them: they will still be 'body warm' and creases won't get set into the fabric.

Do not hang your coat over the newel post at the bottom of the stairs unless you want a hump-shaped sag at the shoulders! Use a coat hanger – a sturdy wooden one is best for coats so they don't sag at the shoulders under their own weight!

Button up shirts at the neck to stop them flopping open and creasing on the hanger. Use trouser hangers unless you really want a crease across the knees of your trousers! Do up the zips to keep them in shape. Hang skirts up by the tapes/ribbons as these stop unsightly bulges at the seams. If your skirt does not have these, use a trouser hanger to grip the waistband.

Drawer Storage

Keep your drawers tidy: do not overfill them. Place often-worn garments in the upper drawers and heavier or less frequently worn garments in the lower.

Wrap silks, cashmere and other delicate materials in tissue paper: this keeps out the light that can otherwise fade the garment and it stops any accidental snags to the fibres.

Absorb any moisture in drawers or wardrobes with a bundle of school chalk tied with a pretty ribbon!

Ironing & Mending

Our clothes are a major investment and we should look and feel good in them every time we put them on. A crisply ironed shirt, no matter how old, will always look good. Missing buttons on shirts, or hems that hang down on skirts or trousers, look like you do not care about details. Anything beyond repair needs to be removed from the wardrobe: but remember that old t-shirts make excellent dusters, cotton shirts can be cut into squares for patchwork quilts or hankies, and hand-knitted jumpers can be 'un-knitted' for their wool.

Ironing

Dry as a Bone

Even when clothes feel dry out of a dryer or off the line, they still have residual moisture in the seams and where the fabric is thicker, around cuffs and collars. Ironing freshly laundered clothes will remove any last traces of dampness as well as remove creases.

An Order to Ironing

Let your iron heat up for a few minutes before using and sort your laundry into piles: one pile for items needing a hot iron, one for a warm iron and a third for a cool iron. For the latter, remember that once you have switched your iron off, it can be used on delicate items that need a low heat, thus saving energy.

Ironing Tricks

Fabric shine – especially on black garments – can be unsightly: iron them 'inside out' and avoid ironing over fastenings, hems and seams. Press embroidery or velvet on the reverse side through a thick cloth – such as a towel – to stop the fibres being crushed. Slip a length of cardboard inside a tie to prevent the imprint of the fabric behind it appearing on the front. You can do the same for pleats on a skirt to stop the fabric underneath the pleat becoming shiny.

Use a reflective ironing board cover – it saves energy and time. Alternatively, slip some kitchen foil shiny side up underneath your ironing board cover to reflect heat upwards.

A Clean Iron

Keep the plate of your iron clean: pass it over a sheet of paper sprinkled with salt. And to keep your iron limescale free, use water that has been boiled and cooled, and always empty the iron after use. If you do get a limescale build-up, fill the iron with white vinegar and turn up the heat to the steam setting. The vinegar will loosen the limescale. Switch off and cool down and empty out any remaining vinegar. Re-fill with boiled water and repeat to remove any residue.

Repair & Maintenance

Buttons and Zips

Secure loose buttons before they drop off and get lost! If you do lose one from the collar or front of a shirt, take one off from close to the bottom of the shirt so you do not have an odd button on show. And do not forget to replace the button at the bottom – keep the spare buttons and yarn that come with new garments for such emergency repairs. Sticky zips can be 'unstuck' by rubbing a bar of soap over them.

Cuffs and Linings

Repair frayed cuffs on jumpers: darn the edges using a small blanket stitch. You can match the colour of the darning wool to the jumper or use a contrasting colour for effect.

Look to your linings: a worn lining means that the inside of the garment will also start to wear. Repair linings where possible, or ask your dry cleaner or local seamstress or tailor to replace the lining for you.

Boots and Shoes

Get shoes and boots re-heeled before they get so worn down that the heel stack is damaged. To help them keep their shape, stuff the legs of boots with rolled up newspaper or magazines and use shoe trees in shoes. If shoes or boots get soaked with rain, stuff them with newspaper to absorb the moisture while keeping them in shape.

Brush suede shoes and garments in one direction only, otherwise it will look shaggy. Shiny, matted suede should be rubbed in one direction with a piece of coarse sandpaper.

Stop patent leather shoes (and handbags) from drying and cracking by a frequent wipe with petroleum jelly finished by a buffing with a soft cloth.

Salt Removal

Salt from winter roads that have caused surface stains on shoes and boots can be removed with a mixture of 1 part washing-up liquid, 1 part white spirit and 4 parts water. Work the creamy emulsion all over the shoe or boot, paying extra attention to the salt line. This will remove any shoe polish and with luck, the salt residue. Rinse off and let dry naturally before re-applying shoe polish.

Energy Saving & Reducing Waste

Saving Resources

Wasting energy not only wastes money but is also harmful to our environment. Gas, oil and coal are non-renewable sources of energy and at some time in the not-too-distant future these resources will run out. What's more, these energy sources are also among the greatest polluters. We must not forget that water is also a valuable resource not to be wasted. Adopting some very simple procedures, such as switching off lights and appliances when not in use, taking our foot off the accelerator or fixing a leaking tap, will save us money and preserve our planet for future generations.

Electricity & Gas

Turn it Off!

Turn lights off when a room is empty and make use of natural light as much as possible.

Appliances such as microwaves, TVs, videos, stereos and computers should be turned off at the socket as they use energy when they are left on standby: it is estimated that 85 per cent of the energy used by a DVD player is consumed when it is not actually in use! Similarly, switch your computer screen off if you are leaving your computer for more than a few minutes as the monitor uses most of the computer's energy.

Unplug equipment like mobile phones, shavers and electric toothbrushes once they are fully charged, otherwise they will keep drawing electricity.

Light Bulbs

If you use a light for an average of four hours or more a day, fit an energy-saving light bulb: it will use around a quarter of the electricity and will last ten times longer than an ordinary bulb. And did you know that light bulbs will last longer if you dust them?

Fridges

Avoid leaving the fridge door open: this raises the temperature (and lets cold air into your kitchen) so the fridge has to work harder to get the temperature back down again. For the same reason, avoid putting your fridge next to an oven or boiler. If possible, keep the freezer in a cool room or garage.

Defrost your fridge regularly to keep it running efficiently and cheaply. If it seems to frost up quickly, check the door seal.

On the Hob

Match the size of the ring to the size of the saucepan or you will be paying to heat the air. The tips of gas flames are the hottest points, so you should only heat the bottom of the pan and not let flames race up the sides. Use a lid on saucepans, so the contents heat more quickly and you use less energy.

Energy-saving Appliances

Pressure cookers, steamers and microwaves do save energy, so add one to your Christmas or birthday present wish list, or check out your local Freecycle scheme for one!

Kettles

Only boil as much water in the kettle as you need as this will use less electricity. If you do boil too much, you could save it in a vacuum flask for doing the washing up!

In hard water areas, you need to deal with limescale to keep your kettle working efficiently for longer. At least twice a year, soak the element overnight in vinegar.

Washing Machines and Dishwashers

Only wash full loads or use a half-load or economy programme. You can also use a low temperature programme: modern washing powders will be just as effective.

With sensible use, modern dishwashers can use less energy and water than washing up by hand. And the tips above apply for dishwashers too.

Heating

Radiators

Foil-back your radiators so that precious heat is reflected back into the room rather than absorbed into the wall.

Extractor Fans

If you have an extractor fan in the kitchen or bathroom, turn it off as soon as it has done its job. Left running for an hour, it can empty a whole house full of warmed air!

Do Not Let Heat Escape

Insulate your home to save energy and reduce your bills. You may also be able to get an energy saving grant to help with the cost.

Make sure curtains or furniture are not in front of radiators and draw the curtains at dusk to keep heat in rooms.

Fit a nylon brush seal or a spring flap to your letter box and put a cover over the keyhole to avoid draughts. Make draught excluders for the base of doors: a tube of fabric stuffed with old carrier bags works well and they can be quite beautiful if you use your creative skills. A short sausage made for the letter box works well too.

A lot of heat energy is lost up the chimney flue so, if you are not using your fireplace, block up the chimney using scrunched up newspaper or an old pillow. This will allow some air to ventilate the chimney to stop damp occurring.

Turn it Down

Turning your central heating thermostat down by just 1°C (2°F) can save up to 10 per cent on your fuel bills. Fit thermostatic valves to radiators: these sense temperature and switch radiators on or off, depending on how warm the room is. The * setting is to protect against frost and will usually leave the radiator switched off unless the temperature falls below about 6°C (43°F). A setting of 3 or 4 should be about right for a normal living room, while for a bedroom 2 is acceptable.

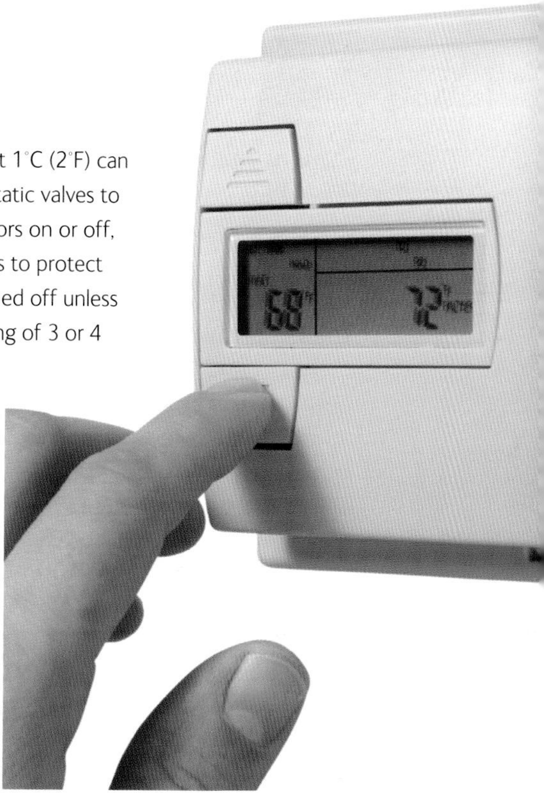

Timing

Do not heat an empty house! Time your heating to go off 30 minutes before you leave the house, and come on again 30 minutes before you are due to return.

Drying Off

Do not put wet clothes to dry over a radiator: this stops the heat from reaching the rest of the room. Try putting up a clothes rail in an unheated room, opening the window slightly to allow the damp to escape and shutting the door to stop heat being drawn into that room.

Water

Change Your Mind-set

Water is a valuable resource, so start thinking of it as a food, rather than something that goes down the plughole!

Take a Shower

Take a shower: a bath uses an average of 80 l (18 gal) of water, whereas a five-minute shower uses just 30 l (6½ gal). However, be aware that power showers use as much water as a bath – and sometimes more.

Sixty is Plenty

Turn the thermostat on your hot water tank down to 60°C (140°F). This is a comfortable temperature for most people for washing and bathing.

Drip Drip Drip

Replace washers on dripping taps to prevent wastage – and stop that drip-drip-drip torment!

Toilet Tricks

'Don't pull for a pee!' Flush the toilet only when necessary. A standard toilet cistern uses 7–10 l (1½–2¼ gal) of water for every flush, which adds up to around 50,000 l (11,000 gal) annually for the average household. The majority of toilet trips probably only require 50–60 per cent of that amount of water for a clean flush. Another way to reduce the amount of water used by your toilet is to fill a large margarine tub, bottle or similar container with water and place it in the cistern. Cistern Displacement Devices or Water Hippos are often available free (or at a reduced price) from your water company. For the actual water that your toilet uses, why not look into installing a device that enables you to reuse grey water (rain, bath or leftover washing-up water) instead of first-class drinking water for flushing your toilet?

Water Meter

The rule of thumb for considering a water meter: if there are more bedrooms in your home than people, a water meter is a good idea. If you know you are a low water user, then you can ask your water company to carry out a calculation for you to see if a water meter would reduce costs further. Want a water meter fitted? Your water supplier may do this for free if your property is suitable. If a meter cannot be fitted, such as in an apartment block with shared pipes, ask the water company to provide you with an assessed charge bill instead of the current bill based on the rateable value of your home.

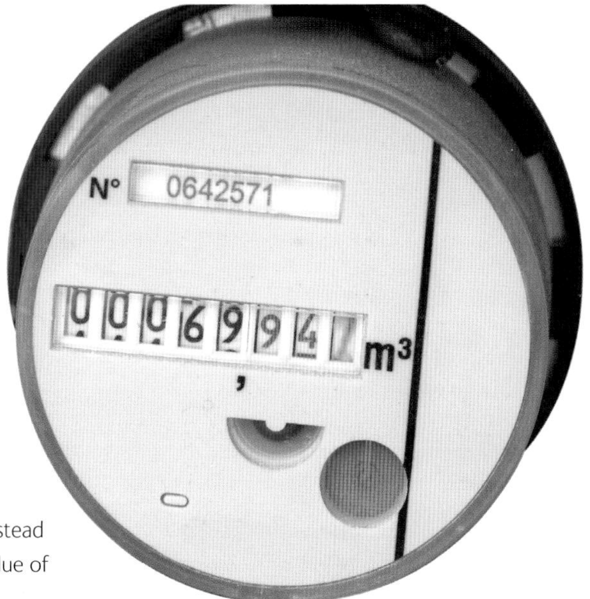

Saving Water in the Garden

Firstly, add a water butt to your garden to collect rain water for watering the garden, or recycle bath, washing-up and shower water on established plants (but avoid water that is heavily loaded with detergents). Then use that water efficiently: watering over the leaves of a plant is wasteful as a high proportion evaporates – water around the base of the plant, and water plants late in the day to avoid moisture loss through evaporation. You can save water by using a watering can or a hose fitted with a trigger attachment as sprinklers are wasteful. Finally, stop the competition for water by removing weeds and put mulch around plants in summer to retain moisture in the soil.

Vehicles

Your Car

Make sure your car is running as efficiently as possible. Have it serviced regularly – an incorrectly adjusted carburettor can waste up to 25 per cent of fuel. And check your tyre pressure: if your tyres are at the right pressure, you will drive more smoothly and save fuel.

Your Driving

Drive more slowly! It can save lives, but will also save you money. For example, you use 30 per cent more fuel driving at 70 mph (112 kph) than 50 mph (80 kph).

Drive more smoothly! Think ahead to avoid sharp braking and rapid acceleration. It saves fuel.

Use your gears as efficiently as possible. You will use a quarter less fuel doing 40 mph in fifth gear than in third!

Switch Off

Switch off! If you are idling while waiting or in a traffic jam you are getting zero miles to the gallon. So, switch off if you can – and that applies to the air conditioning too. If you must use air conditioning, do so carefully, as this increases fuel consumption by 15 per cent.

Wind Resistance and Weight

Cut down wind resistance by removing roof racks and other accessories when not in use: a fully loaded roof rack increases consumption by 30 per cent. Travel light! If you don't need it, don't take it.

Think Before You Drive

Plan your journey! There is no surer way to waste fuel than by getting lost. And if you can, share your trips: if you can share a car, you will save emissions and share the cost. Finally – don't drive if you don't have to! Where possible, walk, cycle or use public transport.

Reducing Waste

Around 50 per cent of a typical household bin's contents can be recycled and another 20–30 per cent can be composted. Yet currently around 85 per cent of our annual household waste still ends up in landfill sites. The mixture of different materials accumulating in these sites often leads to surrounding land and water supplies being polluted. The combination also releases toxic gases into the atmosphere. By recycling waste, we not only reduce the volume of material sent to landfill, but also reduce the amount of energy used to manufacture new products from raw materials.

Creating Less Rubbish

Long Lasting

Buy durable rather than disposable products. Avoid single-use, disposable cameras; use a digital camera instead of traditional film. This will save you money in the long run.

Junk Mail

Avoid junk mail: remove yourself from mailing lists, sign up for the Mail Preference Service, return any unwanted mail to the sender and recycle the rest.

At the Supermarket

Avoid over-packaged single servings, buy your fruit and veg naked (without packaging, that is!) and say no to carrier bags! Use reusable cloth shopping bags instead.

Refill

Wherever possible, buy refills of products such as washing powder, herbs and salt. Drink tap water rather than buying bottled water: refill the fancy bottle from the tap – no one will ever know!

Battery Power

Hundreds of millions of disposable household batteries are bought every year and they generally end up in landfill sites. Use rechargeable batteries instead. For an even greener solution, invest in a solar-powered battery charger. It can be used around the home and can also be taken out on the move to recharge camera or MP3 player batteries. You can also now buy USB batteries which plug into your PC and charge up using your computer's power while it is on.

Save Ink and Paper

Only print when you really need to – if you do print, use both sides of the paper; use cloth handkerchiefs instead of tissues; and next Christmas, agree to send e-cards instead of paper ones.

Do it Yourself

Make your own sandwiches rather than buying shop-packaged ones. By making your own lunch you could also save more than £4 a day (or about £1,000 a year!). And try this at the coffee shop: refuse disposable coffee cups – take your own mug and ask for it to be filled!

Rethink Gifts

Instead of giving disposable goods, give your friends and family tickets for events and activities, such as films or concerts, as gifts .

Recycle

Think Before You Buy

There are more than 4,500 products made with a recycled element: make these your first-choice purchases.

Local Recycling

Make best use of your council's household recycling scheme: recycle your glass bottles and jars, metal cans, plastic bottles, textiles and shoes, newspapers, waste paper and cardboard.

Re-use

Re-use plastic containers (such as margarine tubs) for storage or putting packed lunches in. If you had to get a plastic carrier bag at the shop, use it as much as possible.

Give and Take

Instead of heading out on a spree, swap clothes with friends to cut back on shopping. And don't forget libraries – to borrow books and rent the latest DVDs rather than buying them.

Join your local Freecycle scheme, where you get to give away goods that you no longer need, or pick up great finds for yourself – it all helps divert items from landfill. Visit www.freecycle.org.

Rehome unwanted items by donating clothes, books, CDs and bric-a-brac to your local charity shop instead of throwing them out. Put your old mobile phone to good use: Oxfam, ActionAid or Rainforest Concern will recycle and re-sell them. You can even donate your leftover paint to a suitable scheme, give your old spectacles to a good cause (many high street opticians have joined the World Vision scheme to save eyesight in developing countries) and pass glossy magazines on to your local doctors' or dentists' surgery.

Sell It

Clearing out the attic? Why not try selling your stuff rather than taking it to the dump? Have a tabletop or garage sale or, for more the more desirable or valuable items, put them for sale on eBay.

Repair & Restore

New Lease of Life

Don't dump out-of-date, tired or worn furniture: strip off varnishes, repaint or recover, or just change knobs and handles to give it a new look.

No Excuses

Hire tools or borrow from friends or family for odd jobs, rather than buying your own. Need a repair but cannot fix it yourself? Join a time or skill bank where you can swap your time or skills for someone else's.

Prevention

Make routine maintenance checks: go round your home and inspect for damp, leaks and draughts – and deal with them. Gas boilers need servicing once a year by a qualified and registered professional. If you catch problems early there is more chance of fixing rather than replacing, and reducing waste.

Don't Let it Rust Away

You can easily clean rusty tools by rubbing or soaking them in full-strength vinegar to dissolve away the rust. Or dip a peeled potato in bicarbonate of soda and rub the rusted area (keep dipping the spud in the bicarb!). Alternatively, clean rusty tools with a soap-filled steel wool pad. Dip the pad in turpentine and rub the tool.

Prevent small garden tools from rusting by storing them in a bucket of dry sand, and oil garden machinery and tools before putting them away for the winter.

To remove rust on your car or on other metal pieces, rub a piece of aluminium foil over the area and the rust will be gone!

Scratch Away

Scratches in light-coloured wooden furniture can be removed by using 250 ml/8 fl oz/1 cup lemon juice and 120 ml/4 fl oz/½ cup vegetable oil. Rubbing this mixture on scratches will hide them, making your finish look great. Light scratches in dark wood can be rubbed over with an almond. For deeper scratches, match a child's wax crayon to the colour of the wood and fill the scratch with this.

Hole in the Wall

White toothpaste makes a great filler for small holes made by nails in walls – and it smells minty too! Another trick is superglue – this will make an extra strong wall filler for small holes and indentations if mixed with bicarbonate of soda. Place a few drops of superglue (fluid not gel) in the hole/indentation and, while wet, add bicarbonate of soda. Then add a few more drops of superglue. This will set and become extremely hard – hard enough to drive a nail into! (Be careful: a chemical reaction takes place immediately and creates a lot of heat in a very short time.)

Unstick It

Puff a little powdered graphite into a jammed or stiff lock. Keep all locks running smoothly by using graphite every six months. Avoid using oil: this tends to gum up the works of a lock.

Compost & Wormeries

Why and How?

About a third of all household waste is organic, so if this is recycled as compost, you are reducing the amount of waste sent to landfill. You can build a compost heap and cover it over with some polythene or cardboard. However, bins do look neater and are easier to manage. You can build your compost bin or buy one from any number of suppliers. Contact the Waste and Recycling Department of your local council or authority, who should be able to provide and deliver one.

Location, Location, Location

Locate your compost bin in a sunny or semi-shaded position, directly on the soil or turf and away from watercourses.

What to Bin...

You can compost most household waste, including fruit and vegetable peelings, tea bags and leaves, and coffee grounds. You can even compost cereal packets and egg boxes, waste paper and junk mail, including shredded confidential waste. A paper shredder helps to speed up the process!

For best results, use a mix of fast- and slow-rotting matter in your compost heap or bin. Grass clippings and soft young weeds rot quickly. They work as activators (getting the composting started) but on their own will decay to a smelly mess. Older and tougher plant material is slower to rot but gives body to the finished compost, and usually makes up the bulk of a compost heap. Woody items decay very slowly: they are best chopped or shredded before being added to the heap.

...and What not to Bin

Some items are best avoided: meat, fish, dairy and cooked food will attract vermin and should not be home-composted. Do NOT compost: coal and coke ash, cat litter, dog faeces or disposable nappies.

Wormeries

Easy-to-use, wormeries convert organic kitchen waste into a bio-rich, high quality compost and concentrated liquid feed. You can run a wormery whatever the size of your garden – and even if you do not have a garden. Some wormeries are designed to be sited indoors as they are odourless and hygienic. A wormery not only produces top-quality, fine compost, but it also generates concentrated liquid fertilizer. This can be used as a liquid feed (usually diluted with water) for outdoor and indoor plants, thus reducing the need for chemical fertilizers.

Decorating & Maintenance

Redecorating

The interest in home decoration fuelled by books, magazines and television means there is now a vast range of decorating materials in an enormous range of colours, all designed for the DIY market. It has also meant that the once closely guarded trade secrets of professional interior designers or painters and decorators are now available to everyone. So, whether you live in a tiny terrace or a magnificent mansion, you can decorate your home to make it unique and modern, or restore it to its original historic splendour.

Painting

Preparation

Wash walls from the bottom upwards and make sure your wash each wall in one go – do not stop to answer the phone or the doorbell or you will leave a dirty tide mark that is nearly impossible to remove and difficult to disguise.

Cover door handles with kitchen foil or a polythene bag and mask off light switches and windows with low-tack masking tape to prevent painting them as well! And make sure that paint will not be spread across all the floors throughout your home by keeping a pair of old shoes handy for painting: take them off and leave them by the door, inside the room you are working in.

If you have to paint pipes that are fixed to a wall, cut out a piece of cardboard, place this behind the pipes to be painted and then paint in the usual way. This will prevent any paint getting on to the wall behind.

Getting Started

Wipe the top and sides of the paint can free of dust and dirt so it does not get into the paint when you open the lid. Prise the lid off with the side of a knife blade or paint-can opener – do not use a screwdriver as you will buckle the lid so that when it is replaced there will not be an airtight seal. Then stir liquid paints with a flat, clean wooden stick, making sure you stir right to the bottom of the can. This way, the pigment will be thoroughly blended.

Brush Tips

Rub the bristles of new brushes in the palm of your hand to remove any loose dust and bristles. Dip only the first third of the brush into the paint container. Overloading a brush causes paint dribbles and the bristles are ruined if paint is allowed to run into the roots. It is also an idea to keep a set of brushes (or pads and a roller) for use with white paint only. This will ensure that no coloured paint will be deposited on new white paintwork.

Use a Paint Kettle

Decant paint into a smaller paint kettle. To keep the kettle clean (and avoid old paint contaminating a new colour), line it with kitchen foil (or clingfilm). When you have finished with one batch of paint, you can simply remove the painty foil and re-line the kettle with new foil. Tie a piece of string across the top of the paint kettle and use it to wipe excess paint from your brush rather than on the side of the kettle, thus avoiding nasty dribbles.

Top to Bottom

Rooms are painted from top to bottom: start with the ceiling, then the walls. Next come doors and window frames and lastly, skirting boards. When you paint walls with a brush, start at the top corner of the room. If you are right-handed, work from right to left.

Using a Roller

Use zig-zag strokes when using a roller, covering the surface in all directions. Do not let the roller spin at the end of a stroke, or you will spray paint all over the floor or adjacent surfaces.

Taking a Break

If you need to take a short break between painting sessions, wrap brushes, rollers and pads in clingfilm, a polythene bag or kitchen foil so they do not dry out.

Thin Your Gloss

After a while, gloss paint starts to go thick and is harder to paint with. Add a generous squirt of washing-up liquid to the paint. Give it a good stir and it will go further, spread better and will not leave brush marks.

Wallpaper

The Right Pattern

Large patterns seem to reduce space in a room, while small patterns on a light background make a small room appear bigger; stripes look best on even walls and where a picture rail or cornice provides a break between wall and ceiling; and small, random patterns will help disguise bumpy, uneven walls lurking beneath.

Prepare the Wall

Wash previously painted surfaces first and allow to dry before hanging paper. Cover grease spots (common on kitchen walls from cooking and from hands on stairway walls) with PVA first to stop the grease bleeding through new wallpaper.

Lining a wall first ensures a professional finish (you can also use lining paper to provide an even surface for emulsion paint). Unlike the wallpaper, lining paper is hung on walls horizontally. On ceilings, hang lining paper across the width of ceilings and the wallpaper along the length.

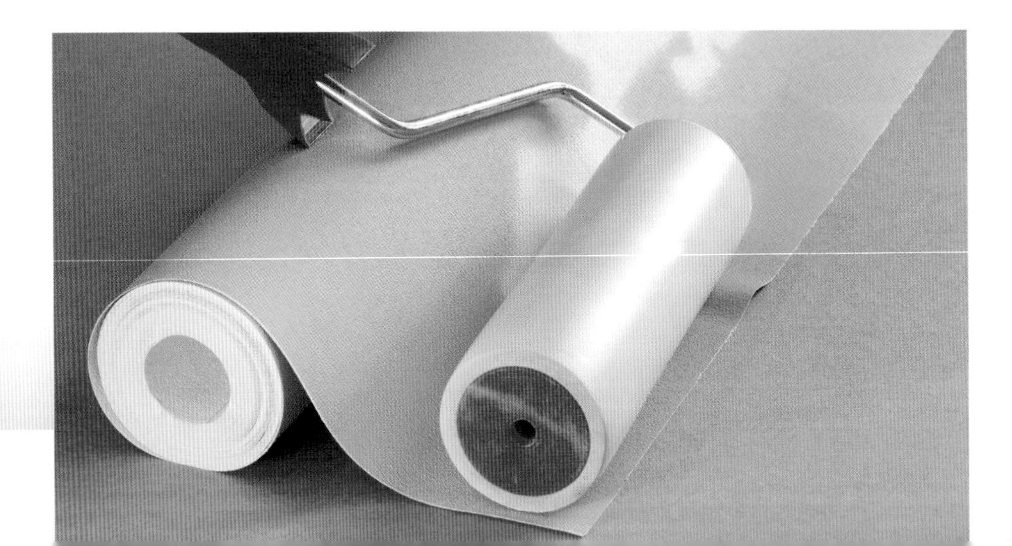

Strip-ease

Vinegar also makes a great solvent for wallpaper paste: add 250 ml/8 fl oz/1 cup white vinegar to a bucket of hot water – as hot as your hands can tolerate – and apply generously with a sponge. Once you get an edge or corner of the wallpaper to lift, start working the vinegar solution behind the paper to break down the adhesive. Rinse your sponge often and mix a new batch when it becomes cool and/or murky.

Wallpaper Blips

Remove air bubbles from wallpaper by cutting into the bubble with a sharp blade, inserting some paste into the hole with a syringe and then flattening to the wall. If you have to repair damage in wallpaper, use a piece of paper slightly larger than the hole and, to get an invisible join, do not cut the paper, but tear it away from you to 'feather the edges'. Paste the new piece over the mark matching the pattern exactly.

Cleaning & Storing Materials

Don't Hang Around

Brushes should be cleaned at the end of each day, and not left standing in a jar of solvent for several days. As for tools, wipe off excess paint with newspaper and run rollers over sheets of newspaper to deposit excess paint.

Water-based v. Solvent-based

Brushes, rollers and pads that have been used with water-based paints should be cleaned with soap and water. Suspend the tools in a warm solution for a few minutes but do not cover the wooden handles of brushes, as this will cause them to swell and eventually split. Brushes used with solvent-based paints need suspending in a jar of white spirit or proprietary brush cleaner. Do not let the bristles get squashed at the bottom of the jar; instead, drill a hole through the handle, insert a long nail through the holes and suspend the brush in the jar. Finish cleaning with soap and water.

Preserve Their Condition

Rinse clean brushes in cool water and give them a final treat with a dollop of hair or fabric conditioner to keep them in top condition. After rinsing, leave brushes, rollers and pads to dry by suspending them from their handles. For even further conditioning, work a few drops of baby oil into clean, dry brushes to keep them soft, ready for their next use.

Turpentine

Put any dirty turpentine into a screw top jar and leave somewhere safe. The colour will eventually drop to the bottom of the container leaving clean turps on the top, which can then be used again.

Stiff and Stubborn

If a paintbrush has become stiff, simmer it in vinegar until it is soft and scrape off the old paint with a nailbrush or wire brush. Clean off in soapy water, rinse and condition and then dry. As for getting paint off yourself: ordinary vegetable oil rubbed well into your hands will remove paint that has dried on your skin more gently than a chemical solvent like turpentine or white spirit.

Paint Pots

Smear a little petroleum jelly around the rim of paint tins before replacing the lids to help maintain an airtight seal. Then, reseal a paint can by placing a piece of stout wood over the lid and hammering down on to it. Move the wooden batten around the rim so the lid is evenly secured.

Paint Imperfections

Drips and dribbles in finished paintwork are generally caused by overloading the paintbrush, while visible brushstrokes are normally caused by poor quality brushes, or because the paint is too thick. When dry, sand back these areas and repaint. Small pimples on the surface of paint mean that there are specks of dust or dirt trapped. Again, sand back the surface lightly, wipe with a damp cloth to remove any remaining dirt and repaint.

DIY

By keeping your home in good repair, you ensure that the fixtures, fittings and equipment also work properly and that long-term and costly repairs are avoided. Most household repairs are simple and straightforward if you deal with them as soon as they are spotted. Most repairs require a little skill, some patience and – importantly – common sense, especially where safety is concerned. If you do not feel confident enough to tackle a repair, or have the time and energy to deal with it through to the end, then call in a professional.

Plumbing

Water Supply

Make sure you know where to turn off the water supply in your home. It is a good idea to turn it on and off occasionally, so that in an emergency, it will turn off easily!

Not sure which direction to turn a tap, stopcock or screw? Then remember this: 'Left is loose, right is tight'!

Pipes

Prevention is better – and cheaper – than a cure! Prevent freezing pipes in winter: insulate pipes with foam held in place with adhesive tape; leave one small light bulb on at night during very cold weather – the heat generated by this is often enough to stop pipes freezing; and try a handful of salt down the drains last thing at night.

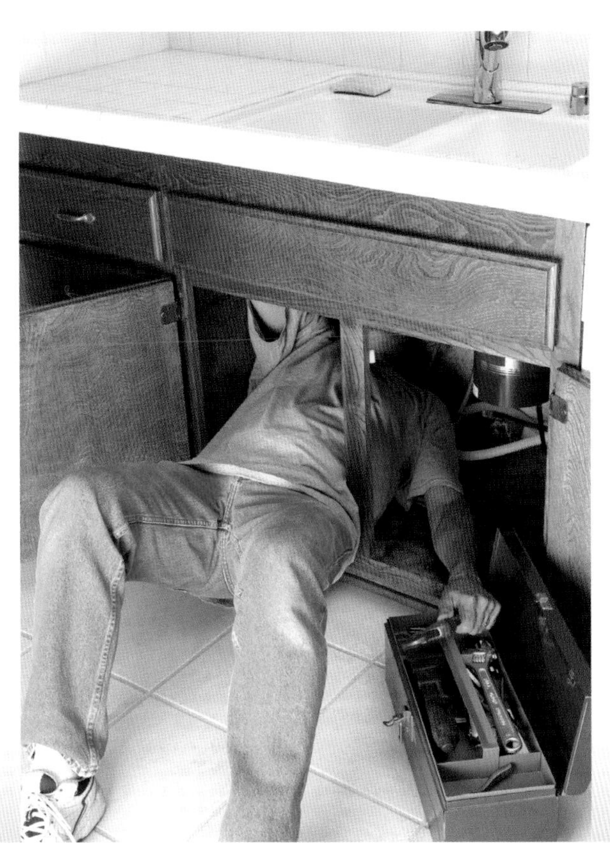

Electricity

Be Careful

Never touch electrical equipment, sockets or light switches with wet hands, feet or cloths – electricity travels through water so you risk a shock. This is well known but often forgotten! To be safe, have any electrical appliances and frayed or worn cords serviced regularly and repaired by a qualified electrician.

Do Not Overload

Do not overload adaptors: you could overload the electrical system. If you smell a 'fishy' or burning odour or a plug feels warm, this could mean an appliance plug is overheating and starting to melt. Switch it off immediately and remove the plug from the socket outlet. Turn off the power at the consumer unit (fuse box) and call an electrician.

Fire, Fire!

Use a special fire extinguisher on electrical fires. If you do not have one, buy one! Get a smoke alarm and make sure the batteries are checked and changed regularly. For a bit of money, your life – and others' lives – can be safeguarded.

Power Cuts

During a power cut, make sure you have some candles and matches ready. Turn off all appliances and lights, apart from one light bulb and the fridge and freezer. A power surge when the electricity supply is restored can blow fuses. When the power is returned, reset electric timer switches and clocks and keep the freezer closed for at least six hours to make up for the earlier loss of cooling power.

Top DIY Tips

Be Prepared!

Be prepared for problems: make sure you know how to turn off the services (electricity, gas and water) to your home; keep a tool kit handy, in good condition and stored where you can get at it easily, ready for action; and, most vital in an emergency, own a good torch – never try to undertake any repair by candlelight.

Nails

Always nail through the thinner piece of wood into the thicker and, where possible, use a nail three times as long as the thinner piece. To stop the wood splitting, do not nail in a straight line along the grain of a piece of wood; stagger the nails instead. If you cannot hold a small nail or tack between your finger and thumb when hammering, push the tack through a piece of cardboard first – hold the cardboard and you will not hammer your thumb. If you need to drive a nail into a plaster wall – to hang a picture, for example – first put a cross of sticky tape on the wall where the nail is to go. This will stop the plaster from cracking.

Nice 'n' Easy

Dip the tips of screws and nails into petroleum jelly or press them into a bar of soap to lessen resistance, prevent wood splitting, stop them rusting and make them easier to remove later if you need to. You can loosen rusted screws or nails by putting a drop of vinegar on their heads and leaving it to soak in. On rusted bolts, try a good coating of cola! And to tighten a loose screw, remove it, glue a wooden matchstick in the hole, then replace the screw.

Drills

A cross of masking tape applied to the surface of a tile, wall or piece of wood is the best way to stop an electric drill bit from slipping off the mark.

Saws

Saw blades glide better if you rub both sides with an old candle, and successful sawing involves applying pressure on the downward stroke.

Sanding

Take the strain off your fingers when you sand by hand: wrap abrasive paper around a small block of wood, or around a piece of dowel if you need to sand in narrow areas.

Squeaks and Creaks

Talcum powder sprinkled into the joints and gaps between floorboards can stop creaks, while squeaking hinges can be silenced with a bit of petroleum jelly, a rub with a pencil, or a bit of washing-up liquid. Cure a sticking door by rubbing chalk down the edge where it meets the frame and close it – when reopened, the frame will be marked with chalk where it sticks and the areas can then be rubbed down with abrasive paper. Finally, sliding doors and drawers will glide more easily if the runners are rubbed with a candle or a little moist soap.

Insulation

If you plan to lay insulating blankets in the loft, do not open the bags until you get them up there. They are specially packaged and, once opened, they expand enormously! Once in the loft, wear a dust mask and gloves as insulation materials can cause skin irritation. And do not forget to lag the cold water tank and the pipes leading from it to prevent it from freezing – in the UK, it's the law! Never place any insulation material directly underneath the tank: the small amount of warm air rising up through the house is needed to keep the tank frost free.

Car Maintenance

Most modern cars generally need very little attention between trips to the garage but a daily routine safety check before you set off, especially if you are driving on the motorway or on a long journey, is a good habit to get into. Cast your eye over the tyres, looking for signs of wear and check that your lights and wipers are working. Getting your car serviced regularly is the best way to avoid problems and, importantly, keep it safe and roadworthy. And keeping your car's service history up to date can help retain its value.

Prevention Better than Cure

Look under your car and look for any fluid leaks, the most common failure in cars. Because a car needs all its fluids, when there is a leak, the leaking part can fail. It is cheaper to have a leak fixed than replace a failed part. Equally, try to get any bodywork damage fixed right away, otherwise rust can set in.

I Can See Clearly Now

Windscreen wash is probably the only fluid likely to need topping up between services. Buy some from the garage, mix with water according to the instructions on the bottle, then use your car's handbook to find where to pour it in. Your windscreen wipers should be changed once or twice a year, depending on their usage. Check them for splits and tears.

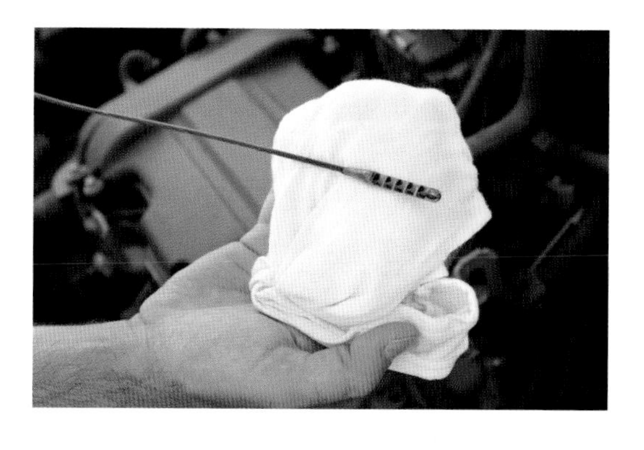

Get Your Hands Dirty

Check your oil once a month. Park on a level surface and wait until the car has been stationary for five minutes so the engine is cool. Pull the dipstick out, wipe it with a clean cloth, stick it back in and remove again. Make sure the oil level is above the minimum mark and below the maximum mark. If the dipstick indicates a low oil level, top up accordingly with the correct grade of oil – check your vehicle handbook. Look carefully at the oil in your car: it should be clean and the colour of dark honey. If it is black or sludgy, has bits in it or a white froth, you might have a problem and should go to a garage.

Keep Cool

Coolant is easy to check as most cars have a clear reservoir under the bonnet with high and low markings, and you should top up accordingly. Check coolant levels before setting off on your journey, particularly in the summer when levels can drop more quickly, causing potential overheating.

Tired Tyres

Under-inflated tyres can also use up to 3 per cent more fuel so it pays to check your tyres regularly! The correct pressures will be in your handbook, but are also on the tyres themselves, and often on a label usually found in the area where the driver's door closes. Top up with air at least once a month, and remember to check the spare tyre too.

All tyres start with a tread depth of 8 mm (0.3 in) but they can wear down differently depending on the car, the roads and the way you drive. The legal limit is 1.6 mm (0.06 in) of tread, but you should make a note to change them when the tread has worn down to around 3 mm (0.12 in). Worn tyres kill!

Safety First

Get a friend to check your car headlights, brake lights and indicator signals to make sure they are all working properly. And don't forget the little lights on the rear number plate! More importantly, brake pads must be checked and changed and your engine checked. Brake pads could get worn down and lose their stopping power, so it is worth paying for a service.

The dashboard warning lights are the car's way of telling you something is wrong: do not ignore them. And join a motoring organization who will rescue you at the roadside should you discover a problem or break down.

Scrub Up

Always make sure that your number plate is visible, especially during the winter when roads are covered with salt, grime and grit. An illegible number plate is a sure-fire way of being pulled over by the police.

Battery

The battery powers the electrics in your car. Driving a car on a regular basis keeps the battery charged. Do check the battery connections, ensuring that they are tight and free from any corrosion.

Outside

Pests & Weeds

One of the joys of having some outside space – big or small – is how it brings us into close contact with nature. The problem with nature, though, is that there are some bits of it we would rather not share! While we all want roses around the door, a striped lawn, to grow prize-winning fruits and vegetables and to be visited by birds, bees and butterflies, we have to remember that next door's cat, the local pigeons (and gulls), greenfly and weeds are all part of the balance (and trials) of nature.

Slugs and Snails

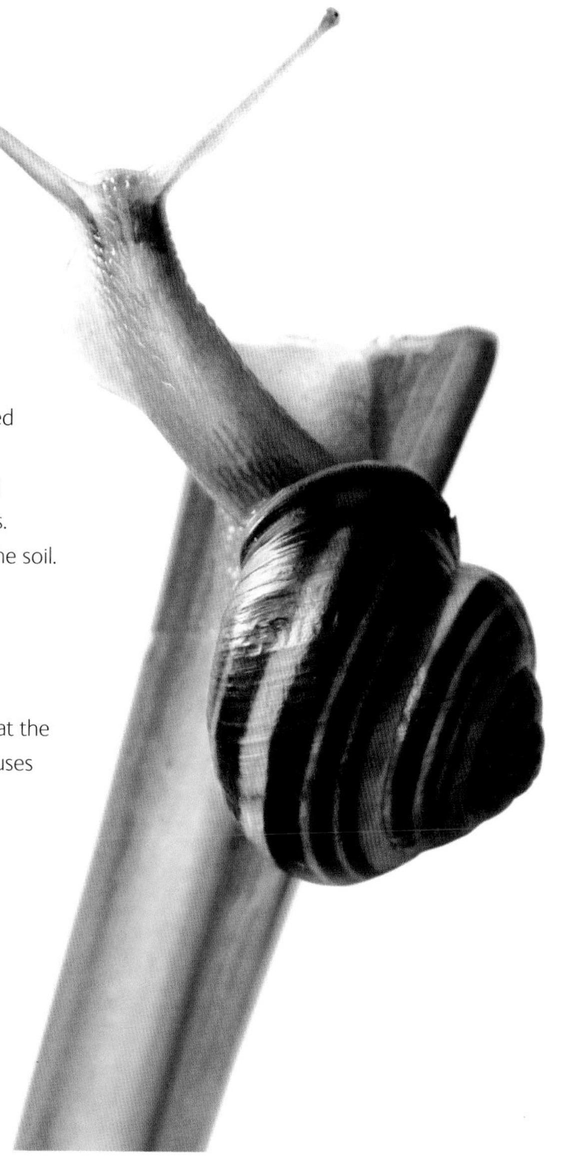

To prevent slugs getting to plants in containers, smear the outside of the container with petroleum jelly or WD40. For plants in beds, bake eggshells in a cool oven to harden them and then place them around the plants; the slugs (or snails) have trouble travelling over the hardened shells. Another way is to fill a small tub (low enough for the slugs to climb into) with beer and place it next to the plants. Alternatively, the tub can be buried in the soil.

Wind Power

A child's windmill (the sort you can get at the beach or funfair) stuck into the lawn causes vibrations that are said to deter moles.

Squeaky Clean

To combat blackfly on runner beans, squirt them with cold washing-up water in an empty washing-up liquid bottle: that way, you can reach the topmost part of the plant.

Ants Away

To get rid of ants, locate their nest and sprinkle a liberal amount of talcum powder around and on it. The ants dislike the talc and will generally move their colony. Continue sprinkling with talc until the ants are moved to where you want them. Stop ants from coming indoors by spraying vinegar around doors and doorsteps. Alternatively, tempt ants with a sprinkling of sugar. When they start taking the sugar back to the nest, mix one part sugar with one part borax crystals. The queen ant will be fed this fatal ingredient.

Nature's Way

Get rid of aphids the natural way: tempt hoverflies into your garden by planting yellow-orange flowers, such as poached-egg plants or sunflowers. The hoverflies will then lay their eggs amongst aphid colonies and gobble up the pesky aphids.

Sneaky Snake

Exploit their aversion to snakes and deter cats and birds from flower and vegetable beds by 'snaking' a small length of hosepipe between the plants.

Dog-gone!

Dogs do not like the smell of mothballs: a few crushed mothballs amongst the plants in your flower bed will send Fido packing!

Tip-toe Through the Tulips

Pets' paws need protection: use liquid chemical solutions instead of powdered fertilizers and weedkillers to prevent pets from picking them up on their feet and then licking them clean.

On the Couch

Couch grass is a nuisance on allotments and, if you do not remove every single root, it will return. Clear couch grass from your plot completely by planting turnip seeds. The two will not mix and the couch grass will wither back and die.

Non-slip Paths

Vinegar kills slippery grass and moss on walks and driveways: spray or pour on undiluted and pull out debris once the weeds have died.

Heave-hoe

Hoeing is the truly organic way to remove weeds: but only hoe the top 1 cm (½ inch) of soil to remove weeds, otherwise you will encourage the dormant ones deeper in the soil to take root!

Plants, Flowers & Vegetables

What grows in gardens depends largely on the type of soil (sandy, chalky, clay), the ability of the soil to drain or retain moisture and its position (sunny and south-facing or prone to cold north-easterly winds). The first two variables can be influenced by the addition of drainage or moisture-retaining mulches and by improving the soil with compost, manure and digging. And, while you cannot change the aspect of a garden, you can choose light- or shade-loving plants that are suitable for your particular situation.

Soil & Fertilizer

Acid or Alkaline?

Some plants like acidic soils, others prefer alkaline soil. (The only exceptions are weeds, which are not at all fussy!) To find out if your garden is alkaline, place a handful of soil into a container and pour on 120 ml/4 fl oz/½ cup white vinegar. If the soil fizzes or bubbles, then your soil is alkaline. Test different spots in your garden as the soil will vary from place to place.

To test for acid soil, mix a handful with 120 ml/4 fl oz/½ cup water with 2 heaped tablespoons bicarbonate of soda dissolved in it. Any fizzing or bubbling this time means your soil is acid.

Bitter Sweet

Keep an eye out for yellowing leaves on rhododendrons, gardenias, hydrangeas or azaleas: this could signal a lack of iron or that the soil's pH balance is above 5.0. Vinegar increases soil acidity (and might be needed, especially in hard water areas): 250 ml/8 fl oz/1 cup vinegar mixed a big bucketful of tap water for watering once a week for three weeks will increase the acidity and release iron into the soil.

Go Bananas!

Banana skins placed around rose bushes will rot down and provide potassium, a vital nutrient.

Go to Work on an Egg

Put broken eggshells into a watering can, fill with water and leave overnight before using. This will extract the nutrients in the shells, making an excellent and cheap plant feed.

Dazzling Daffs

Want your daffodils to be vivid yellow? Mix some dry mustard powder in with the compost when you plant the bulbs.

Plants, Flowers & Trees

Stop the Rot

When growing sweet peas from seed, fill the pot two-thirds with compost and water well, then top up with dry compost and plant the seeds 1.5 cm (1/2 in) beneath the surface of the compost. This way, the seeds will draw up as much water as required and will not rot away.

Seeds, not Sweets!

Some seeds are highly toxic: laburnum seeds, foxgloves and yew berries, for example, are poisonous and should not be grown if there are small children around who may ingest them.

Safety in Numbers

Grow varieties of plants that require little or no staking and plant closely so they support each other.

Lovely Leaves

Liquid tomato feed can scorch the leaves of plants. To stop this happening, pour from the watering can using a piece of 3 cm (1 1/4 in) drain pipe as a funnel directing the feed straight to the base of the plant, away from the leaves.

It's a Jungle Out There!

Before you buy a shrub, bush or tree, do read the label to find out its spread and height. A small shrub or tree can become a huge plant in just a few years, so make sure you plant it in an appropriate place: somewhere where it will not affect your (or your neighbour's) light, view or fabric of the house.

Cutting Your Losses

If a particular species of plant, bush or tree has died, do not plant the same species in the same spot: it may have been affected by a disease that will continue to affect the soil in the area.

Bare Bones

Twisted roots stunt growth so, when you plant bare-rooted trees and shrubs, spread the roots out like an umbrella. As you cover the roots with soil, shake the plant from time to time to allow the soil to drop down well between them, then water well.

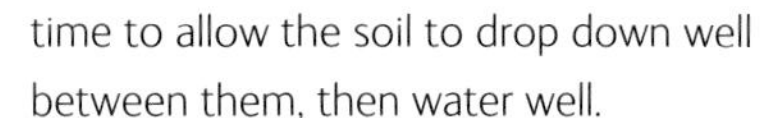

Flexibility

If you have deliberately chosen light- or shade-loving plants to suit your particular situation, you can put them in tubs (or even containers on wheels) so that they can be moved into sunny, shaded or protected spots, as the seasons dictate.

Fruit & Vegetables

Gone to Seed

Starting fruit and vegetables from your own seeds collected from the previous season makes economic sense – even if it takes a little longer to get a crop. Germinate the seeds between some wet coffee filters to check the germination rate. Then, when you plant up the sprouts into pots, put a wet coffee filter in the bottom: this will hold in the compost, yet let the water seep out gently.

Speedy Sprouts

Some woody seeds like gourds, pumpkins and sunflowers can be encouraged to germinate if you rub them gently between some fine sandpaper and soak them overnight in 500 ml/ 18 fl oz/2 cups warm water and 120 ml/4 fl oz/½ cup cider vinegar. After soaking, take the seeds out, rinse them and plant them up.

Fruit Baskets

You do not need a garden to grow fruit and vegetables: tomatoes grow well in hanging baskets (well out of reach of slugs!) and you can grow herbs, salad leaves, garlic and even smaller varieties of carrots in sunny window boxes.

Peas in a Pod

To prevent peas being eaten by pests, fill a short length of guttering with compost and sow peas along the length as normal. Hang the guttering out of reach of pests and, when the seedlings are 3–5 cm (1–2 in) tall, dig a trench in the garden and transfer the whole length, containing compost and seedlings, into this trench.

Evening Shade

In hot weather, water plants, fruit and vegetables in the evening so it has a chance to soak into the soil and reach the plants' roots instead of evaporating into the air.

Mighty Mint

Mint is a vigorous herb, strong enough to break through plastic plant pots! Planted directly in the soil, it will grow... and grow and grow, and take over the whole space. Plant mint into terracotta pots to contain their roots; you can sink the pots into the ground if you like.

Containers

Container Companions

Plants, like people, like company! Group pots and containers together for greater visual impact. You can also make pyramids of pots, raising centrally placed pots on some bricks and grouping smaller pots around and below.

Disguise Drainpipes and Defy Gravity

You do not have to plant leggy climbing plants to disguise unsightly drainpipes: Spanish Rings are plastic rings that attach to drainpipes and have a loop for plant pots to be supported in them. Drainpipes can be festooned with flowers, but do use a soil-less compost so there is no undue weight on the pipework! Alternatively, fill up the legs of old nylon tights or stockings with soil-less compost, tie up the ends, place a loop on them and plant them up as a long, narrow hanging basket: they look terrific on fence posts!

No Heave-ho

Position large tubs and containers before you fill them with soil, compost and plants, or they wi'll be too heavy to move,

Magic Moisture

Mix perlite in with the potting compost in patio planters and hanging baskets. It absorbs moisture when water is plentiful and releases it when the compost is dry.

Drain Away

Before filling a barrel or other large container with compost, stand a piece of drainpipe or cardboard tube upright in the centre and fill with pebbles. As you fill with compost, gradually remove the tube, thus releasing the pebbles. This will act as a central drainage system, preventing the soil from becoming waterlogged.

Know their Place

Save wooden ice-cream spatulas, lolly sticks or plastic knives to use as garden labels. Write on them with a ballpoint pen or waterproof marker.

On the Rocks

Water hanging baskets by putting ice cubes on the top of the soil: moisture is slowly released as the ice cubes melt. Ensure these do not touch the plants, as this may cause damage.

Easy-lift Bulbs

Plant bulbs in a buried flowerpot which can then be lifted when bulbs have finished flowering and the leaves have died down.

Lovely Leaves

Leftover dregs of beer (that have not been used for getting slugs drunk) is excellent for cleaning the leaves of house plants.

Tonic Tips

To help house plants look healthier, mix 1 teaspoon Epsom Salts into 600 ml/1 pt/2½ cups of water. Soluble aspirin in the water also promotes new growth.

Lawncare

Love Your Grass!

A beautiful lawn is a pleasure to behold, but it takes time and dedication beyond the occasional mowing! To keep a lawn healthy may, depending on your soil and your climate, require fertilizing, top dressing, aerating, and/or weed and moss control. It will also need watering, but there may be restrictions during droughts on the use of sprinklers and hosepipes. So, before you lay a lawn, be sure that you are prepared to work at it! And do not forget the lawn clippings: they need to be removed to discourage the spread of invasive weeds.

Slippery Slopes

Mow across a slope rather than up and down. You will have better control of the mower and will be less likely to fall towards the mower.

Lush Lawns

Mowing and fertilizing lawns stimulates grass growth. So, the more often you cut it, the healthier your lawn will be! Mowing little and often is a good way to maintain a good looking lawn. Ideally, you should remove no more than a third of the length of the grass blade each time you mow. In winter, an occasional cut is recommended just to top the grass, keeping it neat and tidy.

Green Lawns

For killing moss and fertilizing the lawn, mix 9 l/2 gal/4 qts water with 90 g/3 oz/½ cup sulphate of ammonia and 30 g/1 oz/⅛ cup sulphate of iron (both available from garden centres). Mix a small quantity of warm water in before adding to the bulk of the water. Use a watering can with a fine rose to apply to the lawn and wet well. The moss will turn black and die within a few hours and the grass will start growing in a few days.

Feed Me!

Feed your lawn at least twice a year to keep it at its best. Use a proprietary brand from your local garden centre and follow the manufacturers' instructions.

Get to the Roots

Grass roots grow in a matted fashion, so once a year lawns require aerating using a fork to spike the grass at regular intervals across the lawn.

Deep Freeze Seeds

When you need to re-seed an area of lawn, the night before, pop the seeds into the freezer: the temperature 'shocks' the seeds into waking up!

Garden Furniture & Hardware

After a hard day's work in the garden, there is nothing better than sitting back in comfort to relax and enjoy the peace and sunshine, feasting your eyes (and stomach!) on the fruits of your labours. But, like the garden itself, the furniture, decks, paths and barbeque equipment all need caring for if they are to look good, last a long time and be safe to use. Secure and tidy storage is essential for garden tools, chemical fertilizers and cleaners, and for over-wintering garden furniture so, before you buy anything, make sure you have space for it, in and out of the garden!

Furniture

Mildew

Wooden garden furniture is very attractive but in warm, damp conditions, mildew can be a problem. Keep a spray bottle of neat vinegar handy: spray on and wipe off the mildew; the vinegar will stop it growing back for a while. For large areas, such as decking, use neat vinegar in a bucket and a stiff broom to scrub off mildew.

Sunshades, garden umbrellas and awnings can also be prone to mildew, especially if they have been packed away and stored through the winter. Clean and deodorize using a mixture of 250 ml/8 fl oz/1 cup white vinegar, 2 tablespoons washing-up liquid and a bucket of hot water. Wear rubber gloves and give them a good scrub before rinsing off with clean water. Open umbrellas, shades and awnings to let them dry off fully.

Are You Sitting Comfortably?

Padded seat cushions on garden furniture are comfortable but they need to be taken in at night to stop them getting damp from rain and dew.

Check garden furniture, especially the hinges and joints, regularly for rust (which can eat through metal and cause bolts to break), and for rotten or splitting wood which may break when you sit down.

Patios & Decking

Clean Sweep

A regular sweep of paved areas and decking with a stiff broom and clean water will generally be enough to get rid of dirt and loose material.

Under Pressure

Pressure washing patios, paths and paved areas is a good way to spruce up gardens after the winter. Be careful not to pressure wash too strongly, especially in the joints between paving stones, as you can break the surface. Every three months or so, inspect pavers and the jointing for cracks, and repair or replace accordingly.

Rakes' Progress

Gravel paths and borders are low maintenance, but not maintenance free! Where there is little traffic, gravel and chippings always seem to migrate to the edges of paths, so you need to rake them back into position. The rake will remove any debris such as twigs and dead leaves and then you can see any weeds popping up in the gravel which can be picked out by hand.

Shiver me Timbers

Like a lawn, decking also requires regular maintenance. Brand new decking will, in its first year, experience a whole range of weathers and temperatures and may end up looking grey as well as dirty. Regardless of whether the decking is of pressure-treated wood (which has a greenish tinge), it now needs a deep penetrating treatment to restore it to its former glory, expel moisture and stop new water from penetrating the wood so that the timbers do not swell, crack and buckle as the temperature changes. Once cleaned off, new decking needs a good treatment with proprietary clear deck oil. Older and stained decking needs cleaning with a stiff brush to work a proprietary cleansing mixture into the wood, hosing down and leaving for 3 days to dry out before treating with protective coats of deck oil.

Hardware

Instant Antique

To age new garden statues, smear them with natural yoghurt. Algae will quickly cover the statue making it look older than it actually is.

Safely Stowed

Prior to storage in winter, drain the petrol and oil tanks and clean the spark plugs of motor mowers. Fill the oil tank with clean oil but leave the petrol tank empty (petrol deteriorates). Leaving a motor mower standing for months on a damp surface or in a damp place will make it difficult to start in spring. Stand it on a piece of cardboard or a block of wood and keep the area as well ventilated as possible to avoid condensation.

Barbecues

Barbecues are great fun and they can be cheap and cheerful (a pre-packed, disposable foil tray with charcoal is fast and fun) or grand affairs ranging from brick-built, permanent features in gardens to professional, gas-fired mega-barbies. Kettle-shaped barbecues are popular: they are lightweight and can be easily stored over winter, but they do need looking after. Make sure they are stored safely in a garage or shed when not in use, or use a fitted tarpaulin cover, otherwise it will fill with rain water.

Shock Horror!

With the power switched off and the tool unplugged, examine electric mower, strimmer and hedge cutter cables for signs of any damage. Any visible signs of wear means these should be replaced immediately.

Oil Slick

Do not turn a petrol mower on its side to inspect underneath: this will result in the petrol and/or oil leaking out!

Over My Shoulder

Use a length of gaffer tape to fasten the cord of electrically powered garden equipment to your shoulder: this will keep the cord off the ground or away from the cutting blades. Make sure electric powered garden equipment is fitted with a circuit breaker; this will cut out the current in the event of the cord being damaged.

Sharp and Shiny

Tools work better and last longer if they are regularly oiled and kept clean and with a sharp edge. To prevent rusting, clean blades and wipe all moving parts of garden equipment with a lightly oiled rag after each use. At the same time, you can check the condition of the blades and cutters to see if they need sharpening, tightening or even replacing. An easy multi-purpose trick is to place a bucket-sized container outside your shed, fill it with sand mixed with some old engine oil (from your mower or even from you car). When you have finished with your spade or hoe, knock off all the soil and then plunge it up and down in the bucket. The result is a well-oiled, clean and de-rusted, re-sharpened tool ready for use.

Food

Culinary Tips

There are plenty of recipe books available allowing us to taste exotic dishes from around the world or enjoy the favourite dishes of celebrity chefs. The best cookery books are ones that share trade secrets or indeed give really useful information about the nuts and bolts of everyday cooking and how to get the best results. Look to your grandmothers' kitchens: here you will find a wealth of information, short-cuts, tips and loads of common sense that are as useful today as they were back then.

Baking

Arise!

Covering rising bread dough with a sheet of greased plastic (an opened-up carrier bag works well) will keep the warmth of the dough just right and encourage it to rise without forming a dry skin.

Crisp Crusts

If you like the crust on your bread to be crispy, brush it with a little salt water halfway through the baking, when the crust has become firm.

A Missing Egg?

If you find you are one egg short for a cake whose ingredients include either self-raising flour or a raising agent, you can replace the missing egg with 1 tablespoon of any type of vinegar. It works and you won't taste any difference!

Sugar, Sugar

Caster sugar is often called for in baking, but there is no need to buy this: make your own by grinding up ordinary granulated sugar in a coffee mill or food processor for a few seconds on a high speed setting.

Dairy & Eggs

Rescue Remedy

Milk that is just about to turn can be rescued with a pinch of bicarbonate of soda. If the milk is too far gone, do not forget that it can still be used for baking the lightest of scones and cakes. If, on the other hand, your milk is fresh and the recipe calls for sour, you can turn the milk by adding some lemon juice or vinegar.

Whipped Up

You will find it easier to whip cream if the bowl and utensils are really cold but, if the cream will not whip into shape, add 1 or 2 drops lemon juice to stiffen it. Whipped cream that has flopped and become watery can be revived by chilling it thoroughly before beating again.

Spread the Calories

Whipped cream and mayonnaise can be made to go further (and be a little less calorific per serving) if you mix natural yoghurt into them.

Hard Cheese

Cheese tastes best at room temperature: store it in a cool dry place or in the fridge but let it warm up before serving. To stop cheese from drying out and going hard at the edges, smear a little butter over the cut sides.

No More Mould

To stop mould on cheese, do not touch the cheese with your fingers but wrap it in kitchen foil or a piece of muslin, along with a few sugar cubes.

More Sherry, Vicar?

Omelettes and scrambled eggs prepared by professional chefs always taste like a dream because they add a splash of sherry. Try it – and taste the difference.

Meat & Fish

T'is the Season

Pepper is a much more expensive seasoning than salt, so always season raw meat and fish first with pepper so it sticks to the flesh. Use salt at the end of the cooking process: adding salt to meat at the start encourages the juices to run, making the meat tough and leathery.

Standing Room Only

Removing raw meat (but not offal, which is more delicate and perishable) from the fridge one hour before cooking speeds up cooking time, makes browning more even and stops the meat from sticking to pans.

Tough or Tender?

Tender meats are best cooked using a dry heat method, such as oven roasting or pan frying. Tough meats, on the other hand, are made more tender if they are cooked using moisture-rich methods, like stewing, braising or slow simmering. You can, however, tenderize meat by hitting it vigorously with a rolling pin (sprinkle this with water first and the meat will not stick to it!) or squeeze a little papaya or kiwi fruit juice over it (both contain the enzyme papain which tenderizes meat).

Up Sticks!

Soak wooden skewers in water for an hour before skewering on the meat, fish or vegetables for kebabs: this prevents the wood from catching fire on barbecues and the moisture is drawn out of the wood during cooking, causing the skewer to shrink, so the pieces of food slide off easily.

Fishy Facts

It is useful to know that: a lobster is really fresh if it has a stiff tail; you can draw off some of the saltiness from anchovies by soaking them in milk for an hour; if you bake fillets of fish on lettuce leaves they do not stick to your tray, and the fillets stay moist as well; if you thread prawns on to skewers lengthways they will not curl up during cooking; and finally, the correct way to eat caviar is on cold toast: hot toast makes the caviar melt and go all runny!

Fruit & Vegetables

Ripe Avocados

Avocados only ripen once they have been picked off the trees: they are shipped in refrigerated containers to stop them ripening, which explains why they are as hard as rocks in the stores! To ripen them up, store them somewhere warm, or place them in a plastic bag with a banana skin.

Tasty Celery

Celery loses its flavour as soon as it is washed: for the best-tasting celery, buy the dirtiest one you can find and do not wash it until you need it!

Gorgeous Garlic

Garlic is a wonderful addition to a dish but it is a bit fiddly to do there and then: have your garlic ready instead by peeling a bulb and popping the cloves into a small jar with just enough olive oil to cover. Not only do you always have garlic at the ready, you end up with a little batch of garlic-infused oil too.

Beans and Legumes

Soak dried peas, beans, lentils and other legumes overnight in water to cut down on cooking times the next day. Unless you are a vegetarian and rely on these as a major part of your diet, it is often more economical to buy canned legumes which are already cooked, saving you time and energy. Incidentally, adding salt to dried peas, beans and pulses at the beginning of cooking will make them as hard as bullets. Add the seasoning at the end when they are tender.

See the Storage section for more great fruit and veg tips!

Canny Cooks

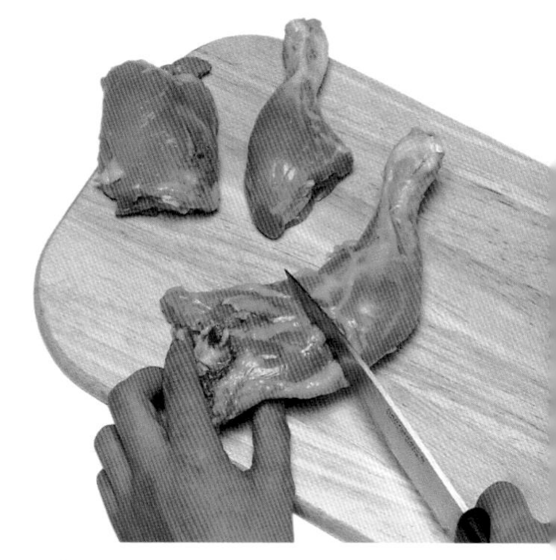

Clean Machine

Wash your hands before handling fresh foods – and wash them again afterwards. Make sure you use separate chopping boards and knives for raw foods and cooked foods, for meat and for non-meat – especially chicken – and do not mix them up.

The Heat is On

Make sure you know what the temperature dials on your oven and hob mean so you cook at the correct temperature: make a chart with equivalent temperatures: for example, a moderate oven is 375–400°F, which is 190–200°C or gas mark 5–6. While you are at it, make a handy chart of cooking times for meat and poultry: how many minutes per pound or kilo, plus how many extra minutes. Doing this will mean that dinner is served at the time you planned and not hours later!

Eat Up!

Cooked food should be eaten and enjoyed while it is still hot, or when it has been thoroughly chilled after cooking. Lukewarm or tepid food is a breeding ground for bacteria, so be cautious of hot dinner canteens, or even hostess trolleys and heated food trays in the home, where the food is kept (hopefully) at a safe temperature by electric elements, night lights or overhead heating lamps.

Storage

Proper storage can preserve food, but will not make it last for ever! Check the use-by dates on tinned, packaged and frozen foods: pin up a list to remind you what needs using up first and, when it is gone, bring the next-in-line forward on your shelves. Food-storage areas need to be kept clean, so once in while (but on a regular basis) empty the shelves and have a good clean-out to remove any odd bits of pasta, rice and cereal that have spilled from their packets, clean up under sticky jars and bottles that have dribbled and make sure labels are legible and cans are not leaking.

Dry Goods

Keep them Airtight

Dry goods like flour, pasta and rice need to be kept in airtight containers to keep them dry. You do not have to decant them from their bags, just pop the whole bag into an airtight jar or container: that way you will still be able to check the measurements, quantities and cooking instructions and see the use-by date.

Canned Food

Canned or tinned foods should be inspected for their use-by date and for any spots, rust or weird bulges in the cans (which means something inside is bubbling away and filling the space with gas. Bin that tin!).

Cans that have been sitting on cupboard shelves will still gather a fine layer of dust on their lids. Before you open any tin, wipe the lid with a cloth so dirt and dust does not fall in when you open it. Alternatively, store all your tins upside down!

Once you have opened a jar or a can of food, the contents will only keep for a limited amount of time. Bottles or jars of food can be stored in the fridge, but they must be considered as fresh food and perishable. Tinned food should be removed from the can and decanted into another container for storage in the fridge.

In the Dark

Do not store herbs and pulses in glass jars because the light permeates the jar destroying the herbs' colour and flavour and toughens the skins on pulses.

Coffee Time

Like ground spices, ground coffee very quickly loses its flavour and becomes bitter, so buy ready ground coffee in small quantities and use it quickly. If you drink a lot of fresh coffee, consider buying a grinder and buying whole beans (store them in an airtight container in the fridge) that can be ground up as and when you need them.

Fresh Food

Little and Often

Fresh fruits and vegetables are best bought in small quantities. Remove them from any plastic wrapping as soon as you can: do it in the supermarket and use their bins to send a statement about over-packaging! Air needs to circulate around fruit and vegetables to prevent them from sweating and becoming soggy. Beautiful as it may be, a fruit bowl is the worst way to keep fruit fresh: use a tray or large plate so they do not touch each other.

Fridge Rules

The temperature inside your fridge should be between 0°C (32°F) and 5°C (41°F). Buy a fridge thermometer as this is the only way to tell if your fridge is running properly at the right temperature. If it is too warm, food will not be chilled thoroughly and bacteria will multiply; too cold and ice particles will form inside the food. And do not overload your fridge! The cold air needs to circulate freely around the food to keep it evenly chilled.

Crisp Lettuce

Lettuce is the exception to the remove-the-plastic-bag-for-storage rule: it seems to thrive wrapped loosely in a bag and kept in the fridge. Revive a wilting lettuce by slicing off any brown from the stalk and placing the stalk in a little iced water. Individual leaves can be revived with a sprinkle of cold water and wrapping in a tea towel in the fridge for half an hour.

Oo-la-la Onions

Onions store well if they do not touch each other and air circulates around them. Make a fake French string of onions from an old clean pair of tights or a stocking: pop an onion in the toe, tie a knot over it, pop in the next onion and tie another knot. Keep on until you put all your onions away: when you need one, just cut the tight or stocking below a knot, et voilà! If a recipe calls for half an onion, use the top half first and save the root end: these keep longer.

Sun-kissed Tomatoes

Some people like their tomatoes rock hard, others like them soft and squishy. Green tomatoes, and those that are not fully ripe, are best stored in a dark place: exposing them to sunlight makes them soft, but does not ripen them. To ripen them, put them in a brown paper bag with an apple, or in a drawer (stalk side up) and leave them until they have turned rosy red.

Melon Scent

Cantaloupe, honeydew, ogen and other yellow-flesh melons should not be stored in the fridge or they will make everything smell – and taste – of melon!

Egg Head

Storing eggs with the pointed end facing downwards on the specially designed shelf in the fridge will keep them fresh for up to ten days. But if you arrange eggs pointy-end downwards in a bowl and place this in the lowest part of the fridge (where it is coldest), they will stay fresh for up to three weeks!

Bacteria Be Gone!

Surface moisture on fresh food is the ideal breeding ground for bacteria, so always remove the packaging from fresh meat, fish and poultry. Pat the surface of the meat or fish dry with a paper towel and place each piece into a separate, closed container or on a plate or a bowl covered loosely with kitchen foil and place in the fridge.

Green Shoots

Although they look attractive, the green leafy tops on carrots, turnips and beetroots continue to draw nutrients out of the root. Trim off the tops and store root vegetables in a cold, dry place with good ventilation. Stop potatoes from sprouting by storing them in a cool, dry place with a few apples and, if you have peeled too many, put the peeled overstock into a bowl, cover them with water and store in the fridge. They will be fine there for two or three days.

Lasting Lemons

Whole lemons keep well for weeks in the fridge if you store them in egg cartons: the less air that circulates around a lemon, the longer it seems to keep. Cut half lemons last longer if you place the cut side down on a saucer or plate and cover them with an inverted glass. If you only need a squeeze of fresh lemon juice, pierce the lemon with a cocktail stick or wooden kebab skewer, squeeze the juice through the hole, then plug up the hole with the cocktail stick or skewer to exclude the air. You will be able to store the lemon for a while this way.

Banish Odours

Vinegar should always be at hand in the kitchen, not just for cooking, but for cleaning and deodorizing. Plastic storage boxes, lunch containers, bento boxes and vacuum flasks can all be stained and tainted by strong-smelling foods: wash food containers in a solution of equal parts white vinegar and water; rinse them clean and store with the lids off. And it is said that if you wipe your hands with vinegar before handling fish or onions, the scents will not linger on your hands.

Shopping

Love it or loathe it, shopping takes time, energy and, of course, money. There is no magic way to make it easier (or cheaper), so you need to find what works for you. That might be shopping daily or doing the whole week's grocery shopping in one. Fortunately, we are well served by shops: supermarkets open late, while local stores can offer variety and service unmatched by many of the food giants. Do your shopping online: although you pay for delivery, it will save you a trip and be delivered right to your door.

Planning

Fill Up Before You Go!

Never go shopping on an empty stomach! You will buy far too much food, including items you want to eat then and there (doughnuts, crisps, chocolate) and end up with lots of goods you do not need.

Happy Meals

Make a plan of a week's menus, thinking about what is in season, on special offer and the nutritional values and flavours of the foods you have in mind. Plan out each day's meals, including packed lunches, so there is a mix of staples, such as rice, pasta and potatoes, fresh (or frozen, canned or bottled) vegetables (and fruits), egg or cheese dishes, with meat and fish dishes bringing up the rear.

Stick to the List

Once you have planned the week's menu, make a shopping list and stick to it! You will save time and money and will not fill your cupboards with unnecessary items. Take a calculator with you too, and keep a running tally of what you have spent as you go along.

Don't Forget Frozen and Canned

Frozen vegetables and canned produce are often scorned and overlooked, which is a shame: the freezers' and canners' facilities are either on farm sites or very close to them, which means that these preserved vegetables are picked and packed at their freshest. There are organic varieties available, as well as those packed without added salt or sugar. However, never buy frozen foods from a freezer that has been stocked above its load line: the uppermost items in the freezer may not be fully frozen and the lower items may have thawed out once and re-frozen. Both are potential health hazards, so avoid them.

Get Packing

Save money and eat like a king (or queen): take your lunch to work. This does not have to mean soggy sandwiches, but pasta or potato salad, some cold meat, perhaps. Make up a lunch the night before, pop it into the fridge and grab it on your way out of the door.

Supermarkets & Markets

Supermarket Sweep!

Get to know the workings of your supermarket: make a note of the best times to shop, including when they make their reductions from the deli and produce counters. Check the use- and sell-by dates on wrappings: if the date is today, ask them to reduce the price. If what you want is not on the shelf, ask for it! It may be in the back waiting to be shelved.

Branded

When out shopping, people automatically reach for the familiar, heavily marketed (and therefore more expensive) brand. Why not swap your usual brand of ketchup, cereal or beans for the supermarket's own brand, which will usually taste exactly the same as the branded version and, nine times out of ten, be much cheaper? And do not sneer at the supermarkets' value ranges, either: there are often great bargains to be had.

Local Markets

Local markets are on your doorstep and can be good value for money. Shop carefully, though: some deals may look like a bargain, but may work out more expensive in the long run. And while the market may be local, the produce may not be.

Market stalls can offer excellent bargains at the end of the day's trading: the stallholders will want to pack up and be rid of the last mushrooms, box of tomatoes or bunches of bananas, which may be at their ripest and ready for eating straight away.

Farmers' Markets

These have sprung up all over cities and towns in recent years: many of the stallholders do indeed offer excellent quality, home-grown or home-reared produce at reasonable prices but remember that the variety of produce on sale will be limited by the growing seasons, so do not expect strawberries at Christmas.

Leftovers

For some reason, many leftover foods taste better the next day. Maybe it is because they have had a chance to rest and the flavours to mature, or maybe it is just because we are hungry and ready to eat anything! Whatever the answer, make it a rule in your house that no food is wasted or thrown away, unless it is unsafe to reheat it or eat it cold. Get your cookbooks out and look for inspiration: many of the finest dishes in restaurants are prepared well in advance and served rechauffé, the posh word for reheated!

Reducing Leftovers

The best ways to reduce leftovers is to plan weekly menus carefully, shop less often, buy fewer products and eat everything. An even better way to deal with leftovers is to stop thinking about them as leftovers and start thinking about them as a whole new meal, or part of a meal.

Cook Once, Heat Once

This is the rule for reheating cooked food: leftovers can only be reheated once. Make sure they are heated all the way through and are really, *really* hot, so any bacteria that has settled on the cold food is killed.

Our Eyes are Bigger than Our Stomachs

If you regularly have leftovers, ask yourself if the portions you are serving are larger than the diners' appetites! If so, then adjust the quantities you are cooking: you will save waste and valuable energy in cooking only what you need.

Wine Cubes

Do not throw away the last remains of wine, freeze it into cubes instead. These are great for dropping into soups and stews to add flavour and it means you do not have to open a new bottle (unless you want to, of course!).

Hot Potatoes

Baking potatoes takes a long time and uses lots of energy: you can speed this up by piercing baking spuds with a long, new nail or by cooking them on a metal skewer so the heat radiates right into the middle. Bake plenty of spuds at a time; any leftover can be cooled and transformed into potato salad, grated into a patty and fried with onions and paprika or mashed and used as topping on tomorrow's shepherd's pie. Because they are already cooked, subsequent cooking times will be shortened.

Crumbs!

Turn stale bread into breadcrumbs: break up the crusts in a blender or dry out some slices in the oven (you can save energy by putting them into an already hot oven that has been turned off). Put the dry slices in a bag and break them into crumbs with a rolling pin. Season them with salt and pepper ready for use on chicken or meat, or freeze them, unseasoned, so you have fresh breadcrumbs to hand whenever a recipe calls for some.

In a Stew

Reheat leftover stews and casseroles by slowly bringing them up to boiling point and cooking them at that heat for at least 10 minutes to ensure no bacteria survive.

Glorious Soup

Home-made soups are easy to make: boil up bendy carrots, the tops of celery, old onions and the odd potato in a pan of water with a stock cube and some pepper. Throw in some pearl barley and cook it all up. Let the mixture cool and then send it for a spin in the food blender. The result: a delicious, thick and warming vegetable soup. No two soups will ever be the same because each time the ingredients are always a little different.

Cherry Ripe

Fruit that is over-ripe, but not rotten, can be transformed into smoothies. Whizz up bananas, oranges, soft berries and tropical fruits in a blender with some natural yoghurt; over-ripe avocados make marvellous guacamole.

Domestic Arts

Organization

Some people seem naturally organized – they are not! Being organized is unnatural but it is essential and can be 'learned'. You do not need military precision for organization – it is your home, not a boot camp – but order and routine will make it safer, more attractive and a nicer place to come home to. You will also save yourself time if you know you can lay your hands immediately on a pen, a pair of scissors, a needle or your passport, and you can save some money too: you will not need to buy a second jar of mustard or spices, for example, if you know you have got some already in your cupboard.

De-Clutter

A Place for Everything...

A common complaint is that there just is not enough storage space in our homes. In reality, there is often plenty of space, it's just that it is full of unused stuff! If you cannot name every item in your wardrobe and drawers, if you have clothes (or worse, food!) that has not been worn (or eaten) for more than three months, if you have gadgets or appliances that do not work, it is time for a clear-out.

...And Everything in its Place!

De-clutter one room at a time and start by clearing the floor and around the edges of the room: do not dive straight into wardrobes, cupboards and drawers, pulling everything out, as this makes more of a mess and will make you depressed! Sort everything into piles of things to keep and things to get rid of.

Put all 'widowed and orphaned' objects (odd socks, the single earring, the bits of plastic and the instruction manuals that came with the stereo/TV/DVD player/computer) into a separate box for re-homing later in their proper place.

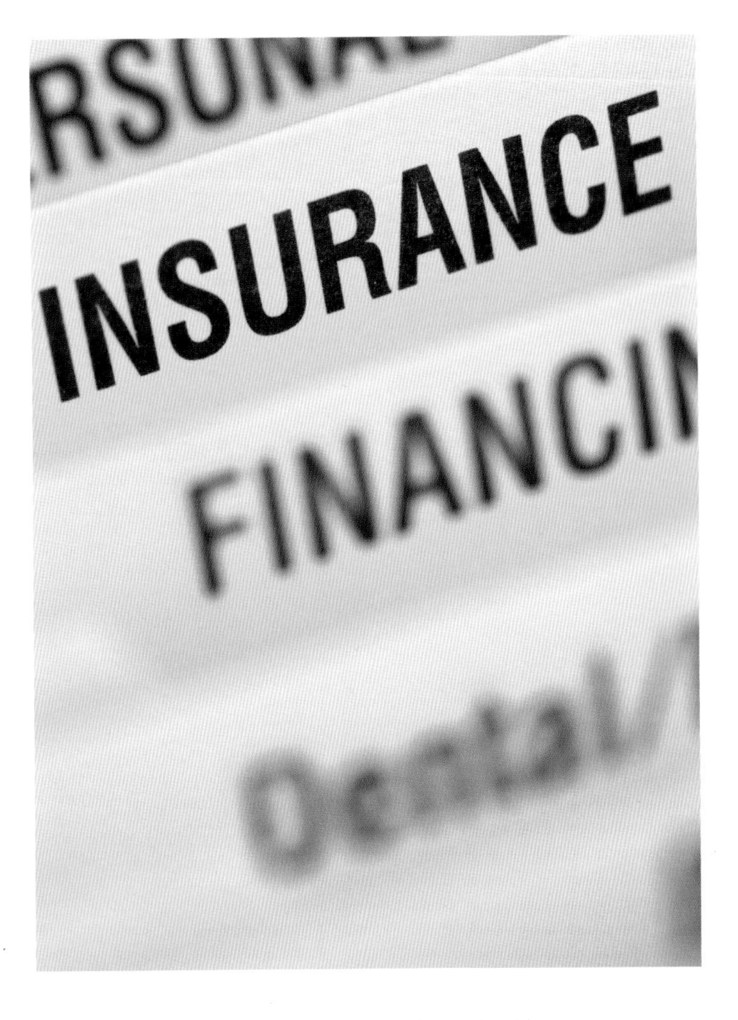

Sorted!

Go through papers and documents slowly and carefully: get some files or storage boxes to keep important documents (insurance and MOT certificates, bank and credit card statements, household appliance guarantees, passports and birth certificates) safe and to hand.

Recycling or Refuse

Anything that you have decided can no longer have houseroom should be recycled: give wearable, clean clothing and books to charity stores; donate furniture and (working) electrical appliances to a housing charity. Anything that is of no use to man nor beast should go in the bin. If you share your home, make sure you do not bin other persons' items of emotional or sentimental value, no matter how much they annoy you.

Planning

Diaries v. Calendars

Diaries are very useful in reminding you what you have to do *today*: planning ahead and knowing what you are doing tomorrow and the days after tomorrow is much more useful. Buy a calendar or a year planner and on it mark all the important events. Use one colour for personal events (birthdays, anniversaries, days off) and another for important household events (motor and household insurance renewals, gas boiler safety inspections, etc). This way, you won't have to cancel dates because the car's in for a service!

Got Your Number!

Write down important telephone numbers, addresses, contact names and reference numbers in a notebook. If you write down the make and model of your printer and the ink cartridge it uses, you can safely throw away the box it came in!

Picture This

Most people have a digital camera, so put it to some very good use: go around your home and photograph all valuable items. Save the pictures on to a CD or print them out and place the information into a file with your household insurance documents. If anything is ever stolen or damaged, you can show the police or insurance company exactly what was what.

Kitchen

The Incredible Bulk

Bulk buy offers may save you money, but have you got space for two dozen tins of beans, 10 kilos of rice, or a year's supply of cat food? Never assume bulk buying means each item costs less than if bought singly: take a calculator with you so you can work out unit prices.

Stock Taking

When you bring tins and packages home from the shops, write their 'use by or 'best before' dates clearly on them. Rotate your stock: put the most recently purchased packages and tins at the rear of the cupboards and bring older products to the front – and use these first. Do the same with the contents of your fridge.

Wrap and Stack

Raw and cooked foods must be stored separately in the fridge: wrap and stack foods so the juices of raw meats do not drip on to cooked food. Keep meat and dairy produce separate too.

Eat Up!

In an ideal world, no household or individual should *ever* waste any food. Eat up everything, but not if it has grown its own fur coat, moves of its own accord, smells off or unusual in any way, is discoloured or has unusual coloured blotches or white spots, or has long passed its 'use by' date.

See pages 126–135 for more tips on food shopping and storage.

Bedroom & Bathroom

Rise and Shine

On average, our bodies secrete about 300 ml/½ pint/1¼ cups of moisture each night which all gets absorbed by your mattress and bedding. Throw back the covers and let your bedding air off for 20 minutes before making it. Duvets need airing every day: drape them over a chair or, in summer, over a clothes line to let the flattened filling expand and dry out. Like duvets, pillows can be aired outdoors on a clothes line.

Turn Over

Turn over your mattress, or reverse the head and the foot ends, regularly (about every three months, but more often when it is new). This keeps the stuffing even and distributes the wear. Foam mattresses generally have a layered construction and should not be turned, but they can be reversed head to foot.

Dust and Debris

As well as moisture, we lose a lot of dead skin which, along with dust, tends to accumulate in mattresses. Use a vacuum cleaner on a light setting for foam mattresses, but use a brush on sprung and other types of mattress to avoid dislodging the layers of padding beneath the mattress covers.

Towels and Sponges

Hang up towels after use: leaving them in a wet heap on the floor will keep them damp and encourage bacteria and mould to grow – and they will smell disgusting too. Natural sponges and loofahs need to have a bath of their own once in a while: if they are slimy or dried out and dusty, soak them in salt water to clean and revive them.

Dude, Where's My Car?

Believe it or not, a garage, if you have one, is where cars are kept safely off the road. Garages are not storage facilities, but they can legitimately be used for drum practice. If your garage is so full you can't fit either the car or the other band members in, then you need to clear it out.

On the Shelf

Garages are really useful for storing things like tins of paint, oil, tools, chemicals and cleaners out of the house. Put up some strong shelves to keep things off the floor, make sure everything is labelled and that there is a good, bright light in the garage to see everything by.

Attic Attack

The attic is a 'storage black hole': it is where things disappear into and are often never seen again. Do not fool yourself into thinking there is a forgotten Titian or Turner masterpiece up there: it is more likely to be the junk we had no use for but which we thought 'might one day come in handy'. It won't, so it's time to get rid of it. Make sure the loft ladder is secure, and that there is enough light for you to see what you are doing. Get someone to help you just in case you get trapped up there! Make sure you walk only on the rafters and not between them, unless you want to come through your bedroom ceiling. Use the opportunity while you are in the attic to check the roof: can you see daylight through it? If so, you need the roof fixing!

Homemaking

Welcoming friends, neighbours and relatives into our homes strengthens family and social ties, and it gives you a chance to show off too! You do not have to have grand dinners for a hundred of your closest friends: a cup of coffee and a chat is often all that is needed. The only danger in being a good host or hostess and having a comfortable home that people love visiting is getting guests to go home! Do not be afraid to tell them 'the party's over', but do tell them they will be welcome again another time.

Entertaining

Clear the Scene

Tidy away clutter and anything that is valuable or breakable! Make sure any dirty laundry is well out of the way. Make sure there is plenty of loo paper. And, if possible, put the cat out if it has a habit of walking across tables, licking plates, making those gagging noises under people's chairs, or flirting with the guests who are allergic to/hate cats.

Plan Ahead and Keep it Simple

If you have invited friends round for dinner, plan what you will be serving well in advance. Forget about doing flambéed dishes: go for a menu that can be pre-prepared, heated up and served easily, otherwise you will spend the entire evening in the kitchen and never see your guests!

Brilliant Buffets

Buffets are a great way to entertain, especially if your guests are a mixed bunch of vegetarians, carnivores and omnivores. Make big bowls of salads and cold pasta dishes, provide plenty of bread and let them help themselves!

Can't Cook, Won't Cook?

This does not stop you entertaining! Ask friends to each bring a dish: you provide the drinks and the plates. Paper ones are fine.

Scented Scenes

If you are happy for your guests to smoke in your home, help minimize the smell of cigarette smoke by discreetly positioning a saucerful of vinegar somewhere in the room. Cat litter also works well, but is even less romantic and elegant! To make rooms smell fragrant, throw citrus peel on to an open fire or boil a small pot of water and add a few drops of vanilla essence, lavender oil or a cinnamon stick.

Lighting & Candles

Shine a Light

Pools of light from small lamps dotted around a room make it look cosier and more intimate than a single, bright ceiling light.

Lasting Flames, without Smoke

Candles will burn for longer if they are cold: put your candles in the fridge before a dinner party. And candles will not smoke so much if you dip the wicks in vinegar and leave them to dry before lighting. *Keep candles well away from curtains and soft furnishings and do not leave them burning unattended.*

Sparkling Eyes

For the most flattering effect, the flames of candles should 'dance' at eye level: all your guests will look gorgeous. Avoid intimate dinners *à-deux* with little tea lights set on the table: they cast their light upwards, causing shadows on your face and make you look like you starred in the *Blair Witch Project*!

Flowers for the Home

At the Florist

Choose flowers that are still in bud as they will be the youngest in the shop! Check also that the stems are not mushy below the water line. And do not buy flowers on Mondays: if you do, haggle on the price as they are normally left over from Saturday's delivery! Ask for your flowers to be wrapped in paper, not cellophane. While the latter looks glamorous, it acts like a sauna. It dehydrates the flowers to the extent that it can halve their lifespan. Paper is also much more environmentally friendly.

Preparation for the Vessel

Short-stemmed flowers do really well if you stick their stems into a bowl of wet sand instead of a jug or vase of water. If you are using a vase of water, strip off any leaves that would be below the water line in the vase, otherwise they will rot and kill the blooms.

Revivers

If you cannot change the water in a flower vase every day, pop a piece of charcoal or a copper coin into the water instead. If a dwindling bunch of flowers looks a little forlorn, do not compost them yet, just bulk the display out with some greenery. Parsley, lavender and rosemary look – and smell – terrific.

Fighting Flowers

Even though they might look gorgeous in a vase, some flowers just hate being with others: keep tulips, daffodils, carnations and nasturtiums on their own in separate vases! Sweetly scented stocks are the serial killers of the flower world: their leaves rot quickly and poison the water for other flowers! Buy them when they have tight buds. Break (do not cut) the stems between two nodes and let them sit in a bucket of cold water before arranging them.

Friendly Foxgloves

Foxgloves are very companionable flowers; in fact, they will prolong the lives of other flowers in the same arrangement.

Sensitive-stemmed Gerberas

Geberas' stems rot very quickly under water. Do not give them a long cool drink; instead place them in a jug or bucket with 1 cm (½ inch) of boiling water for a couple of hours to stiffen their stems. And only fill their vase with water up to ⅓ of the length of the stems.

Twisting Tulips and Looping Lupins

Both these flowers continue to grow when cut, which is why they twist and turn out of position after you have carefully arranged them! Nevertheless, treated well, they can last for ages: they love a good sugary feed so dissolve a good tablespoon of sugar in 500 ml/18 fl oz/ 2 cups of water, cut each stem to the required length and then pour some of the sugar solution up each stem and plug the cut end with a little ball of cotton wool! Fiddly, yes, but it can make hollow-stemmed flowers (including delphiniums) last for weeks. You can also 'tickle' tulips into shape: gently stroke the stems into your preferred position!

Health & Beauty

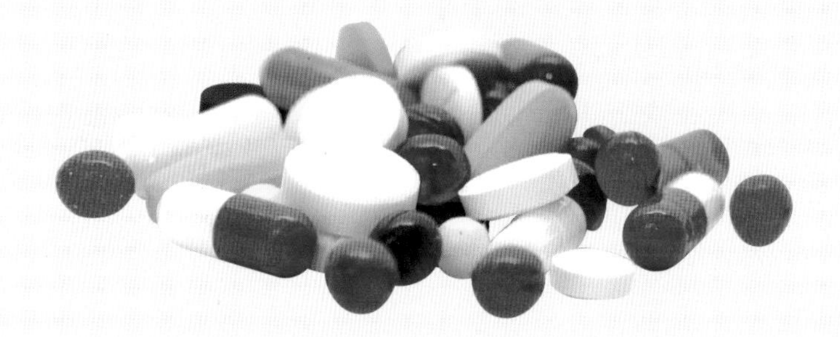

Appearance

Men and women, young and old, all want to look good from head to toe. But no matter how much time and energy you spend on hair and beauty products, or how many you use, they will never compensate for a bad diet, too many late nights, not enough fresh air and exercise, nor will they deal with the ravages of smoking and drinking alcohol! So, if you want to improve your looks – and your health – look first to your diet and lifestyle!

Face & Skin

Clear Complexions

The easiest way to clear skin is to drink plenty of water! But it is also a good idea to consider your diet and your exercise (or lack of it), as well as those late nights out!

Face Facts

It helps to know what type of skin you have: wash and rinse your face and then pat dry with a towel. Wait two hours, then press a paper tissue against your face. If the tissue comes away evenly covered in grease, you have oily skin. If there are grease marks where your forehead and chin came into contact with the tissue, you have combination skin. If the tissue is unmarked, then you have normal skin, but if your face feels taut, then you have dry skin.

Hey, Good Lookin'! (What Ya' Got Cookin'?)

For dry and sensitive skin, chamomile cleansing milk is ideal: heat 125 ml/¼ pint/½ cup creamy milk and 2 tablespoons dried chamomile flowers in a bowl over a pan of simmering water. Simmer gently for 30 minutes, then remove the bowl from the heat and let it stand for 2 hours before straining. Decant into a bottle, label and date it, and place in the fridge where it will keep for a week. Apply to the skin with cotton wool. For oily skin, use the same quantities as above but substitute buttermilk (or natural yoghurt) and crushed fennel seeds.

Witch(hazel)craft

Neat witch hazel is an inexpensive and mildly antiseptic toner that you can buy from your local pharmacist. One of the oldest skin toners known to womankind is made using 3 tablespoons rose-water (which softens the skin) and 1 tablespoon witch hazel. Blend in a bottle and shake well before use. The recipe is good for normal skins; for greasy skins use equal proportions. For dry skins mix the rose-water with 1 teaspoon runny honey.

Cool Cucumber

For a toner for oily skins, whizz up a good chunk of peeled cucumber in a blender, strain the pulp by pushing it through a tea strainer with the back of a spoon, then mix the cucumber juice with a few drops of runny honey and stir well. Store in the fridge where it will stay fresh for up to a week and dab it on after cleansing your skin.

Steam Clean

Steaming your face opens pores and encourages the skin to let out impurities. Fill a bowl with hot water, lean over and cover your head and the bowl with a towel to stop the steam escaping. Adding herbs to the hot water makes for a pleasant and very effective deep clean: fennel removes impurities; rosemary is good for deep cleansing; lavender, rose petals or thyme for gentle cleansing; sage is great for oily skins; parsley for dry or sensitive skins; and dandelion is great for more mature skins.

Smooth Away Wrinkles

Want smoother skin? Quit smoking and drinking! Alcohol dilates the blood vessels, opens pores in the skin and reduces muscle tone; smokers have more (and deeper) wrinkles than non-smokers.

Razor Rash

A terrific way of dealing with itchy, irritated skin and getting vitamins A, D and E (the magic ingredients of many expensive face creams) is to eat an avocado. Then, after you have enjoyed this super fruit, rub the inside of the skins over your face and neck. Leave the avocado on your skin for a few minutes, then rinse off.

The Eyes Have It

After a long day, tired eyes can be relieved by lying back, closing your eyes and popping a slice of cucumber over each eyelid.

Hair

Crowning Glory

If the water you use in your final rinse is tepid rather than warm, it will encourage the hair's outer cells to lie flat, giving your hair a smooth, shiny finish.

Shine Out!

Just 1–2 tablespoons vinegar added to your hair rinse water will remove any lingering shampoo residue and give your hair a terrific shine.

Bright Blondes

Blonde hair glows even more if you dunk a chamomile tea bag in boiling water, let it cool and add the liquid to your hair rinse water. Repeat with each wash to really see the difference.

Red Alert!

Enhance the natural red tones in brown hair by boiling up some ordinary onion skins in water, strain when cool and add the liquid to the final rinse. Leave the onion water in your hair for a few minutes, then dry as normal. The results do build up after a couple of washes.

Sun-kissed Hair

Add that 'sun and surf' blonde look to your hair: just squeeze a lemon, brush the juice into your hair and let it dry in the sun, but do not overdo it, or your hair will become dry and brittle.

Body and Shine

Before your final rinse, try pouring beer – yes, beer! – over your hair. Massage in well, then rinse and dry as normal. You will be amazed at the volume and shine to your hair.

Give Dandruff the Brush-off

A terrific tonic for hair (that also prevents dandruff and hair loss) is made by boiling up a big bunch of stinging nettles in 500 ml/18 fl oz/2 cups water (boiling destroys their sting). Leave the liquid to cool, then rub (leaves and all!) into your hair. Rinse off, then shampoo as normal.

Lush Locks

Not a cure for baldness but for thousands of years men (and women, too) have massaged their scalps with rosemary steeped in olive oil to keep their hair lush and healthy and, it is said, to keep grey hairs away!

Cuts and Combs

Having your hair trimmed every six to eight weeks will keep it in good condition, remove damaged ends and maintain its style. If you have to comb your hair three times a day to keep it in style, it is time to have your hair trimmed! Use a wide toothed comb for de-tangling windswept or wet hair and avoid brushes with densely packed bristles which can pull, stretch and break hair. And remember, too, to clean your combs and brushes!

Hands & Feet

Dirty Digits

Clean stained fingers and hands by rubbing them with the cut side of half a lemon. Cigarette stains can also be removed using this method, but badly nicotine stained fingers need dabbing with 20 volume hydrogen peroxide and rinsing off. Then think about what the cigarettes are doing to your lungs!

Pampered Paws

Hands and feet deserve a treat now and again. Make them feel cleansed, toned and super-smooth with a hand and foot mask. Mix some natural yoghurt and oatmeal into a paste. Apply to your hands and feet (or any part of your body that needs a little TLC) and leave on for 10–15 minutes before rinsing/showering off. You will be amazed by the results!

Itchy Feet

To alleviate itchy feet, add 50 ml/2 fl oz/$^1/_4$ cup cider vinegar to a foot bath and soak your feet well. The mildly acidic vinegar will give foot fungus the boot!

Tired Toes

Seaweed is a wonderful soother for aching and tired feet, so bring some back from your holiday. Alternatively, try a foot bath with added sea salt.

Tea Tree for Toes

Tea tree oil is a powerful antiseptic that is very useful against athlete's foot. Dilute the oil with equal amounts of water or vegetable oil and apply three times a day, directly to the affected parts with cotton wool or a clean cloth.

Smooth Skin

Say goodbye to rough skin on hands and feet (and on elbows, too): mix a little vegetable oil (sunflower, almond or olive oil are all ideal) with granulated sugar and rub vigorously over rough skin for a few minutes. The sugar sloughs off the rough skin and the oil is massaged in. Rinse off and let your hands and feet 'air dry'.

Single File

Do not file your finger or toenails using a back and forwards motion: nails are weakened and split more easily if you do. Start at the outside edge and work towards the middle, doing each side independently. Use an emery board rather than a harsh metal nail file.

Keep Clean

If you are going to do some dirty work, like cleaning or gardening, put a dollop of lanolin or petroleum jelly under each nail before you begin and the dirt and earth will not get stuck under your nails.

Clothes, Make-Up & Teeth

The Brush Off

A good clothes brush is essential: shake out clothes after wearing them and hang them up. Before wearing, give them a light brush to remove dust and hairs (human and pet), paying particular attention to the shoulders and backs of coats and jackets, and the seats of trousers and skirts.

Sheer Delight

Sheer nylon tights or stockings can easily snag, so spray them before wearing with hairspray.

Chill Out

Eyeliners, eyebrow pencils and lipsticks work better, smudge less and last longer if you keep them chilled in the fridge!

Lavish Lashes

Eyelashes look much longer if you sweep the mascara brush towards the outer edges of your eyes.

Pucker Up

Pamper your lips: keep them protected and smooth with a lip balm or a dab of petroleum jelly.

Heaven Scent

Perfumes keep their scent for longer if you store them in a cool, dark place and avoid exposure to the air and light: pop the cap back on bottles and sprays and put the bottle back in the box.

Pulse Points

Perfume scent rises, so the best places to apply perfume are behind your knees and on your ankles. Pulse points, where the blood runs close to the surface of the skin, are warm spots and encourage scents to develop: behind the ears, the nape of the neck, on temples and crooks of elbows are good and, unlike at the wrists, the perfume will not disappear as soon as you wash your hands!

Pearly Whites

The one thing that adds the finishing touch is the one thing you cannot buy: a smile. But you can give your teeth a quick polish by rubbing a strawberry or a sage leaf over your teeth! Chewing a few leaves of parsley or watercress (both are high in chlorophyll, the main ingredient in commercial mouthwashes) will freshen your breath, too!

Brush Away

If you are a heavy tea or coffee drinker or you smoke, occasionally brushing your teeth with a paste made of 1 teaspoon bicarbonate of soda and a little water (you could even add a drop of essential oil of peppermint) will help reduce stains on your teeth.

Home Remedies

While many people swear by folk remedies for common ailments, every home (and every car) should have a first-aid kit for emergency use. There are also a few important things to remember before you use any of the treatments suggested here: first, prevention is always better than a cure; secondly, if you know you are, or suspect that you are, allergic to any of the ingredients, do not use them. Finally, the remedies offered are no substitute for qualified medical advice: serious or prolonged symptoms and illnesses in children must be diagnosed and treated by your doctor.

Headache & Toothache

Massage Relief

Relief from a headache can often be had if you close your eyes, relax and place your middle fingers at each temple, press very lightly and make small circular motions with your fingertips. Repeat the circular massage across your forehead and along your eyebrows.

Coffee and Feverfew

This is an old headache remedy that many swear by, perhaps because it tastes so foul that it takes your mind off the headache: drink a small cup of black coffee mixed with the juice of half a lemon.

Cottage gardens were once full of useful plant remedies: feverfew is a beautiful daisy-like plant that grows happily in any garden, but make sure you know exactly which plant it is. Chew a few of the leaves to relieve a headache; add them to a salad if you like.

Cloves and Ginger

While you wait for the dentist to see you, a drop of clove oil on the affected tooth will provide temporary relief.

Mix some powdered ginger in a little water to make a gooey paste. Dip in a small cotton wool ball, or a folded up piece of clean cotton gauze, and wring it out. Apply the compress to the tooth (try not to let it touch your gums) for relief. If you can stand the heat, ginger and red chilli pepper mixed in the same way is pretty effective on deeper toothache.

Stomach Ache

Indigestion

Indigestion is often caused by hydrochloric acid (which is natural and vital in the process of food digestion) leaving the stomach too quickly. The acetic acid in vinegar can help: 1 teaspoon cider vinegar mixed with 1–2 teaspoons honey in a glass of water taken after a meal is as effective a remedy as any shop-bought preparation.

Burp!

Trapped air (often caused by eating too quickly, or too much at once) can be uncomfortable. The simplest and most effective remedy is to release the air by burping: if this does not happen naturally, help it along by dissolving ½ teaspoon bicarbonate of soda in a glass of cold water. Stir it well and drink it down slowly. Sooner than you think, you will burp and feel much better!

Menstrual Cramps

While menstrual cramps can be exhausting, there is much that can be done to alleviate the discomfort: raspberry leaf tea and strawberry leaf tea can both be effective. Ginger tea (just 1/4 tsp ground ginger in a cup of hot water with a little sugar or honey added, if you like) is probably one of the most effective natural remedies.

Sprains, Cuts & Bruises

Comfort from Comfrey

To reduce the initial swelling of a sprain, apply an ice pack (such as a bag of frozen peas). A loose bandage soaked in comfrey tea can help stop some of the discolouration of bruises, dislocations and sprains. Comfrey contains allantoin, an anti-inflammatory chemical that promotes skin repair; it is also an ingredient in many commercial skin preparations.

Clove Oil and Honey

Cuts need to be washed out first and covered to keep out any dirt. But did you know that a little clove oil (which is antiseptic and a mild pain reliever) dabbed on a cut will help keep it from becoming infected? (It may sting a little at first, though.) Around the world in folk medicine, honey is dabbed on clean, minor wounds because it dries to form a natural bandage. Manuka honey is particularly effective, and is often used in the treatment of ulcers.

Arnica, Parsley and Potatoes

Arnica has pain-relieving, antiseptic and anti-inflammatory properties. Commercial, homeopathic arnica ointments are available but you can also make a healing solution by steeping 1 teaspoon of the dried herb in a cup of boiling water. Steep until cool and then dab on to the bruise with a clean cloth. *Note: arnica should not be taken internally.*

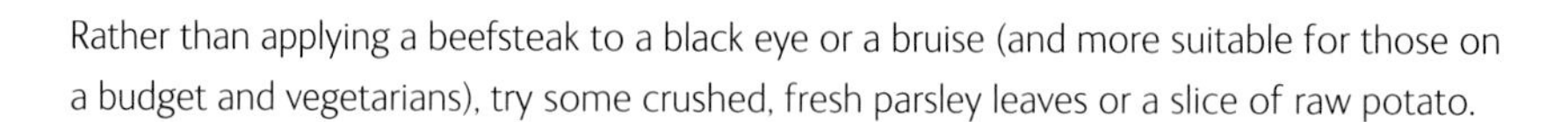

Rather than applying a beefsteak to a black eye or a bruise (and more suitable for those on a budget and vegetarians), try some crushed, fresh parsley leaves or a slice of raw potato.

Stings & Burns

Vinegar for Vasps, Bi-carb for Bees

This simple mnenomic will help you remember which cure to use on which bite! Remove the stinger by scraping the blunt edge of a butter knife along the skin in the opposite direction to the point of entry into the skin. Some swear by the following argument: a wasp sting is alkaline so is neutralized by the mild acid in vinegar, while bee stings are acid and are neutralized by a paste of bicarbonate of soda and water – dab on with a cotton wool ball. Mosquito bites can also be alleviated with a dab of vinegar; some say the smell keeps the mozzies away, too!

Any redness or swelling 24 hours after being stung may indicate an infection, so consult a doctor. If you have had a severe reaction to a sting or bite in the past, you should consult your doctor about the need to carry a syringe of epinephrine (adrenaline) with you at all times.

Airtight

The sting of minor burns can be treated by excluding the air from the affected area. Rinse the burn in cool water as soon as possible, then cover it with toothpaste. Alternatively, keep a little bottle of lavender oil in your kitchen or your medicine cabinet and dab it on to minor burns. The oil keeps the air out and the lavender will aid the healing process and reduce any scarring. Garlic can also be helpful: the Romans applied a paste of mashed garlic (which has antiseptic properties) directly to burns. This protected the wound, kept the air out and probably smelled so much that no one came near you and touched your burnt bits!

Sunburn

Before it starts to sting, cool down sunburn by gently dabbing the affected areas with a cotton wool ball or soft cloth soaked in white or cider vinegar.

Coughs

A cough that is keeping you and the rest of the household awake at night can be calmed very easily: mix 1 tablespoon turmeric powder (which is a wonderful antiseptic) in a glass of lukewarm milk. Add some sugar if you need it. This really works!

Children

Care

Looking after children, nurturing them and watching them learn and develop is a joy, regardless of whether you are a parent or relative, carer or guardian. While there are hundreds of books on parenting, child development and psychology, most of the time, it is practical skills, knowledge – and just plain common sense – that are needed to keep children safe, healthy and happy. Sometimes, just being there to listen to a growing child's concerns is what is needed to set their minds at rest.

Babies

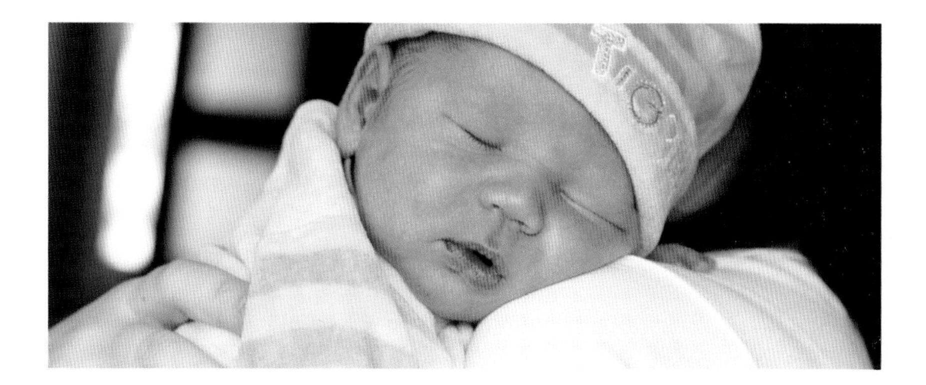

Cry Babies

Babies are pretty helpless and crying is their only way to express their needs. The trouble is working out just what the problem is! Is it wet nappies? Hunger? Wind? Tiredness? If it is a wet nappy, change it! If it is a while since the last feed, then feed it! If it is wind, then lift the baby up and place against your chest and shoulder and gently pat its back and wait for the burp (remember to place a cloth on your shoulder first, though!). Some babies cry when they cannot get to sleep: try stroking the baby gently while talking softly or singing a lullaby.

The Crankies

Over-stimulated, cranky babies respond to background, or white, noise which helps them to focus, relax and nod off! The familiar sounds of the vacuum cleaner, the washing machine or a radio makes a baby feel secure and can help them to sleep.

Nappy Happy

The redness and scaling of nappy rash is uncomfortable and is caused by the wet nappy rubbing against the skin for too long or fitting too tightly. Irritation can also be caused by the soap residues in cloth nappies (and underwear): rinse these in a mild solution of water and white vinegar (abut 120 ml/4 fl oz/½ cup of vinegar to 2.25 l/4 pints/2¼ quarts water) to neutralize the alkaline of the soap and balance the pH level.

Bathing Belles and Beaux

Check the temperature of bathwater with your wrist (it is more sensitive than your elbow) before putting baby in the bath. Never leave your child unattended in the bath, or indeed near any water. Wash baby's face and head first, when the water is cleanest. And if you use baby shampoo, put the bottle in the bath to warm up the contents: cold shampoo can come as a shock!

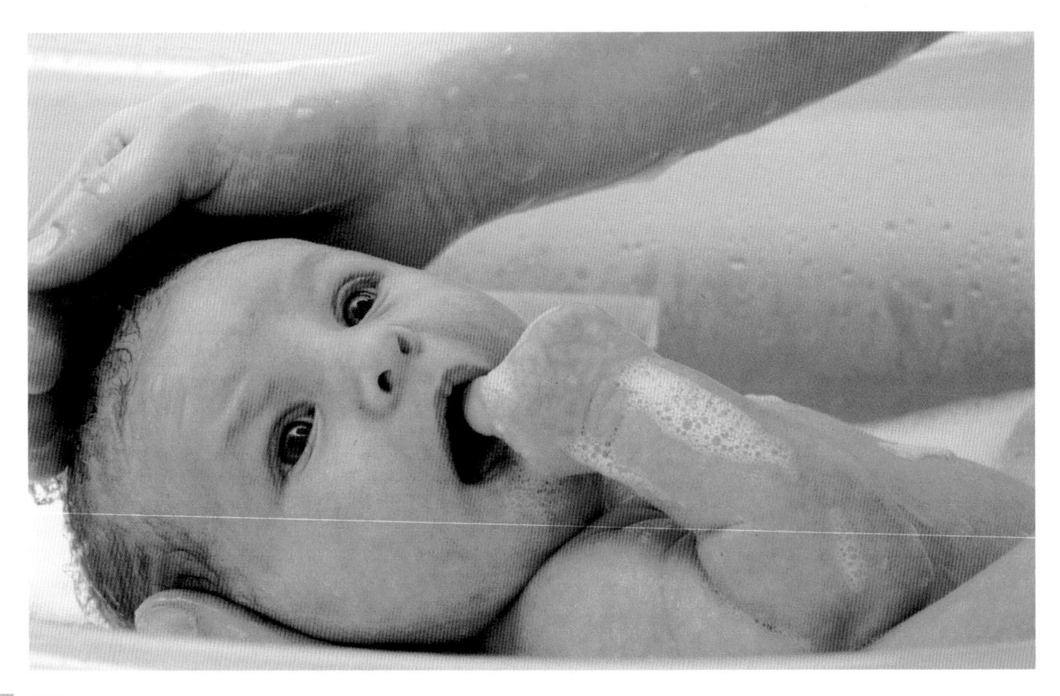

Toddlers

Safe and Sound

Keep medicines and cleaning products in containers with childproof caps and locked away from children.

Mucky Pups!

Teach your children the importance of clean hands, especially after stroking pets, visiting the lavatory and before eating.

Cover Up

Sunburn is painful enough for adults, and we know how to avoid it. Get children to wear a sun hat and make sure to use plenty of sunscreen, paying particular attention to areas that are prone to burning: the back of the neck and knees, noses, cheeks and foreheads.

Older Children & Teens

Emergency Procedures

Create a family accident-and-emergency plan that outlines what to do, who to call and where to go in an emergency. Make sure you and all your family know each other's mobile phone numbers and contact numbers at work.

Food Fads?

Do not make an issue out of any new foods introduced to your kids: let them see you eating it and enjoying it, and they probably will too. But if they hate it, do not make them eat it! If they are not sure, suggest a second bite – maybe with some ketchup if they think it will add to the flavour!

Follow the Leader

Do not fall into the 'Do as I say, not as I do' trap. Instead, do things together: exercise together, wash the car and walk the dog together.

Help with Homework

The fastest way to learn is to teach: if a child is struggling with their homework, ask them to teach *you* what they have learned. Be a patient listener and your kids will often solve tricky problems.

Belt Up in the Back!

Whatever age – no matter how grown up they think they are – do not start the car until everyone has fastened their seat belts, and that means in the back seat too.

Respect!

Teenagers always complain that we treat them like kids, so give them some responsibility once in a while: if you are planning a weekend treat, let the teens know the budget and let them plan the day, reminding them that they have to somehow please everyone! Once in a while, let your teens prepare the meal of their dreams (within budget, of course). The deal is they can have whatever they want as long as they cook it – and wash up!

Have a Girls' (or Boys') Night Out

In spite of what they may say, teenagers do like doing things with their parents, even more so if it is just them with no siblings around. A trip to the cinema or theatre together, a sports event, a gallery or museum is a nice way to spend time in each other's company.

Safe Online

Be open and honest, and talk about going online: most teens are busy chatting with their known friends and updating their Facebook or MySpace entries, but remind them that not everyone online is who they claim to be, that they should not give out personal details or their password, and think twice about posting pictures over the Internet.

Entertaining

You do not need to be a professional entertainer to keep kids amused, their hands busy and their minds engaged; in fact, most of the time, kids entertain themselves. Sometimes, though, it is a real treat for kids to do something with an adult: to paint together, do some cooking together, watch a movie together and laugh together. And, if older children complain of being lonely or fed up, do not forget to remind them of Groucho Marx's words: 'Outside a dog, man's best friend is a book. Inside a dog, it's too dark to read.'

Toys & Crafts

Rejuvenating Playtime

When your toddler has grown tired of a toy, get together with other parents and swap toys, or put old toys out of sight for a while, then magically bring them out when they have been forgotten! And you do not even need toys! A great big box makes a playhouse, a castle, a car or truck, a boat, a hiding place ... all you need is a little imagination.

Magic Painting

Draw a simple design on paper with a white candle. Make up some watery paint in a strong colour and let your toddler paint to reveal the design!

Self Portraits

Get some old wallpaper, roll out a long length with the plain side upwards, then get the kids to lie down on it so you can trace around them. They can then paint or crayon in their features.

Potato Prints

Cut some thick slices of raw potato and then, using different shaped cookie cutters, cut shapes into the middle of the slice. Dipping the slices into thick poster paint and stamping the patterns and colours on to a long piece of wallpaper is great fun for kids.

Memories Are Made of This

Get teenagers to help you sift through family photographs and make albums; they could use their computers to make a digital archive, or get younger children to glue the pictures down.

TV & DVDs

Home Cinema

Toddlers love this: arrange all the chairs in the living room in rows and seat your toddler and all the dolls and teddy bears in the audience comfortably. Turn down the lights and put on a DVD. An interval – for a snack, drink or 'comfort break' – can be added.

Square Eyes

Be realistic when it comes to TV: a couple of hours watching TV or playing on a video game will not harm kids. But do not let two hours turn into six hours.

Make it a rule that the TV gets turned off during homework time: kids will complain, but they will soon become used to the quiet time – and they may even like it!
It does not have to be monastically silent, though: ask how they are getting on and talk about the subject. You can even work together: look things up in a dictionary, an atlas or on the Internet.

Long Journeys

Tune In

Portable CD or MP3 players are great for older children (and teens): they can listen to their favourite music without interference. Younger children or the whole family will enjoy audio books on tape or CD. Or, have a singalong – younger children will love it, and older children will pretend to hate it, but secretly love it – and then join in later.

Plan the Route

Plan a long car journey with several stopping-off points: for leg stretching, for trips to the loo or just for looking at a view. Have some fun with place names: what anagrams can you make from them?

Travel Sickness

Motion sickness can be prevented before travelling by sipping ginger tea or even ginger beer (but make sure it is made with ginger and not artificially flavoured). You can also buy ginger capsules at health food shops. Take along some leak-proof bags and wet wipes, just in case. Get kids to look out of the front windows of cars and not the side windows where the landscape whizzes past in a blur; on boats, they should look out over the stern (the back end) rather than the prow (the front), which goes up and down. Strangely, children are rarely travel sick on trains, so it is worth considering this form of travel as an option.

Party Time

Keep it Simple

Kids' parties can be a nightmare, usually because the children are so stuffed with E-numbers from cakes, crisps and fizzy drinks that they run riot! Plan children's parties carefully and stick to your budget – and do not be fooled by tales of so-and-so's party where there were celebrity entertainers and rides on space ships! For younger children, keep it simple, whether it is at home, in the park or at a child-friendly restaurant – and remember that parents or carers will also be there, so it is a chance for you to make friends too.

Themed Events

Older kids often enjoy a party with a theme: let them decide on the theme, then work out a budget and negotiate on numbers, the venue and time (of arrival and departure).

Teenage Kicks

Sleepovers are great: your home may be invaded by giggling girls or gangling youths, but at least you know where they are, you can keep an eye on them and you know exactly the tricks they get up to – because you did them when you were a teenager! Set the ground rules: no alcohol, no adult-rated movies, no excuses.

Index